Mission in Asia
by Stanley Shenk

Edited by Mark Musselman

Pinchpenny Press
Goshen College, Goshen, Indiana 46526
1988

Credits

Mark **Musselman**, editor, production
Fred **Schlabach**, cover design, illustrations
Printed at Evangel Press, Nappanee, Indiana

Contents

To Doris

Foreword

While I was teaching Bible at Goshen College, my brother Charles, a missionary in Japan, spoke to me several times about possibly coming to Japan for a short-term teaching ministry. Like Mary of old I kept these words in my heart. I knew too that the door was probably open for another teaching term at Union Biblical Seminary in India, where I had taught in 1975-76. Moreover, in the summer of 1984, Charles Christano of Indonesia had invited me to serve in his churches.

As the first year of my retirement approached, the Mennonite Board of Missions, Elkhart, Indiana, and the Mennonite Central Committee, Akron, Pennsylvania, brought all these invitations and openings together and arranged conjointly for a nine-month teaching program (September '85 to June '86) for Doris and me in Asia. MBM sponsored us in Japan and India, and MCC sponsored us in Singapore and Indonesia. At a later point MBM also asked us to spend a week in Burma.

We saw vital congregations, learned to know broad-gauge and attractive mission persons, and worked with eager Bible students. We were both impressed and appalled by elements in the cultures we visited, but we were always fascinated. On several occasions we cast free of our church sponsorship and for days at a time took the tourist trail.

During the nine months I kept a daily journal — people, panoramas, sounds and colors, conversations, incidents, embarrassments, and anecdotes. Some of it is missions and churches — and some is personal adventure, national culture, and the splendor of sea and sky.

This book is a series of excerpts from the journal. But since journal prose is often hasty and unruly, I have rewritten segments. Moreover, lest certain entries seem unduly divorced from context, I have added background. Occasionally too it has seemed fitting to rearrange sequences or expand ideas. And to protect confidentiality, a few dates, places and names have been altered.

Hokkaido

Four Months In Japan

On September 8, 1985 we arrived in Tokyo and spent a week with my brother Charles and his wife Ruth, long-term missionaries in Hokkaido and Tokyo.

For most of our time in Japan, September 15 to December 16, we lived in Kushiro, the largest city of southeastern Hokkaido. I held Bible classes (Jeremiah and Introduction to the Old Testament) in the Tsurugadai and Tottori congregations of Kushiro, and in Bekkai and Nakashibetsu, 50 miles to the north. I also commuted to Obihiro to teach Hebrew Life and Culture and Biblical Archaeology in the Bible school there. And we accepted speaking invitations from Sapporo, Ashoro, Furano, and Asahigawa.

During our last twelve days, December 17 to 28, we were tourists on the islands of Honshu and Kyushu.

September 10, 1985

During lunch two Japanese girls, Tomoko Fukuhara and Fumi Yoshimura, clerks at a Tokyo department store, came up to Charles and Ruth's apartment. Charles and Ruth had said, "Come to see us," and since the girls had a day off, they accepted the invitation. Quickly Ruth made room for them at the table.

Tomoko is an Okinawa girl. A beauty. Vivacious. A marvelously mobile face. Lovely olive skin. High cheekbones. Eyes set wide apart. A flourish of dark hair. She knows very little English, but it was a pleasure just to watch her speak in Japanese. She used little uninhibited gestures — and made a subtle, tiny drama out of choosing a candy square from a dish. She doesn't know how charming she is. Charlie says Okinawa people tend to be less inhibited than the more sophisticated Tokyo-ites.

September 12

In Japan the honorific suffix *san* is usually placed after an adult's last name. Charles Shenk, for example, is called Shenk-san by his neighbors in the Honan-cho community of Tokyo. Seldom in Japan is a man called by his first name. Thus Charles is only rarely spoken of as Charles-san.

In a small church or an intimate social group a woman is often called by her first name. Thus Ruth Shenk is usually referred to in the church as Ruth-san.

September 14

Almost without exception a Japanese word must close with a vowel. This is true even with words imported from other languages. Today at a Tokyo restaurant when I tried to pay with a traveler's check, the clerk consulted by phone with a superior and then said in Japanese to Charlie, "I cannot accept a *checku*." He had to have a *cardo*. So I gave him my American Express *cardo*.

September 16

In late afternoon yesterday we flew 600 miles northeast from Tokyo to Kushiro. At the airport we were met by Genny Buckwalter, a Mennonite missionary here, and Mimoto-san, pastor of the local Tottori Mennonite Church. Within an hour we were in Mimoto-san's home. There we met Chisako-san, his attractive, gracious wife, their two sons, Nozomu and Mitsuru, and their daughter, Yumiko.

While Chisako-san served us dinner, Yumiko, the charming second-grader, sidled up to me and began tutoring me in Japanese from one of her cartoon books. She would shyly point to a picture (house, tree, car, doll, man, woman) and then pronounce the Japanese name. With the aid of such a winsome teacher I began to make a little progress.

Later in the evening Doris and I were taken to our second-floor apartment in Sumiyoshi, only a ten minute walk from downtown Kushiro. Our apartment is very livable, and from our porch we can see both the ocean and distant Akan-Fuji, a perfectly shaped volcanic cone.

September 21

Today I asked Genny for the Japanese words for the numbers one to ten. "In what connection?" she asked. I soon discovered that the Japanese vocabulary is very complicated indeed. It turns out that there are different patterns or endings for these numbers — depending on whether one is speaking of flat, round, long, or pointed objects or books or shoes. And apparently even these categories only constitute a beginning.

When I told Genny that I simply wanted numerals in order to be able to give street numbers to taxi drivers, she gave me *ichi, ni, san, shi, go, roku, shichi, hachi, kyo and ju.*

September 23

After the church service in Asahigawa I stepped into our bedroom next to the sanctuary — and there on the *futon* (a pallet-like bed made up on the floor) was a beautiful Japanese doll, with its eyes closed. But I looked again, and it was a little Japanese girl, fast asleep. A doll, indeed.

September 26

Recently I was talking with an American woman as Japanese children were passing by on their way home from school. She turned toward them and said, "There go the best-dressed, best-educated children in the world." I can easily believe they are the best dressed; they all look as if their outfits were bought yesterday at the best clothing store in town.

As to whether they are the best educated I'm not sure. In Japan the topic of education is discussed endlessly and opinions abound. It is obvious that the education of the young is extremely important here, and that high priority is given to school budgets. It is also clear that students are expected to study diligently, and that parents give strong support to the educational process. I hear reports and read articles however which indicate that rote memorization is emphasized far more than discussion, and that due to the Japanese emphasis on group conformity, a brilliant student is sometimes kept in check lest he out-perform his peers by too wide a margin.

October 1

The northern island of Hokkaido is Japan's frontier; much of it is wilderness and in sharp contrast with the tightly compressed communities, cities, and tiny rice fields in the south. While Hokkaido has some dairy farming (American-style Holstein signs appear along asphalt highways where country lanes lead back to isolated homesteads) and small fields of rice, radishes, beets, and onions, the eye is constantly caught by vistas of clear-running streams, forest reaches, and high peaks and ranges.

People in the southern islands look at their Hokkaido

cousins with ambivalence. These northern Japanese live in a new land — without the cultural riches and ancient associations of Kyoto, Osaka, Miyajima, Nara, Kamakura, and Nikko — and so there is a degree of disdain for the benighted people of the north. But there is also a sense of envy and admiration for the greater social freedom and pioneering achievements of their northern kinsmen.

October 4

Yesterday and today I have seen a large number of fishing vessels anchored and tied up in the Kushiro River just below the big Nusamai Bridge. Usually one sees a dozen or so but now there are hundreds, eight or nine abreast, on each side of the river. Only a narrow lane of water in the center of the river is open. What has brought them all in from the sea? A crisis with Russia over fishing rights? A big fishing industry meeting? A strike? A storm at sea? The last-named is the probable answer, for this afternoon from a high bluff I saw heavy seas crashing against the harbor breakwater.

October 8

Everywhere I go in the little Mennonite congregations I hear about Ralph Buckwalter. He and his wife Genny came to Hokkaido as missionaries in 1951. Although it is commonly said that no *gaijin* (the Japanese word for foreigner — it means "outside person") ever fully masters the Japanese language, Ralph became quite skilled in it. He was tall, and when he lived in Kushiro an acquaintance called him "The Kushiro Tower." He was warm, poised, likeable — a man with a quiet charisma. He liked the people and they liked him. Once a year he and Genny would go to the home of a Japanese friend and help for days in the rice harvest. "It was a therapy for him," a friend told me.

Increasingly the Japanese people looked to Ralph for leadership. He could sit in a conference session and not say a word, but if he finally slightly nodded his head, "the decision was made." He tried not to over-use his leadership potential, and yet of course he did use it. "Things went his way."

During our visit in Sapporo today with Norman and Ruth Kraus (missionaries from Goshen, Indiana) I heard more about Ralph — and also about Takio Tanase. Young Takio was led to Christ by Ralph and Genny in the early 50s, and later attended Hesston College in Kansas and Goshen College in Indiana. This is the story Norman told me: "When I was teaching the Christian Faith course at Goshen, Takio was one of my students. He was quiet. He sat in the back of the room and for weeks said nothing. Then one day he came to me and said, 'I like these lectures; Christianity begins to make sense to me now.'

"'But didn't Buck-san [a shortened, familiar form of Buckwalter-san] and the others tell you these things?'

"'Yes, but it didn't make much sense.'

"'Then why did you become a Christian?'

"'Oh, I didn't become a Christian because of what Buck-san *said*. It was what Buck-san *was*.'"

The death of Ralph Buckwalter from cancer in 1980 was a heavy blow to his Japanese friends and followers.

His memory is revered. In fact, for a time after Ralph's death large photos of him were placed at the front of at least two Japanese churches. Genny, his widow, objected. Only Jesus should be depicted at the front of a church, she said. Her wishes were followed and the pictures were taken down. But pictures of Ralph hang on the walls of many Japanese homes. The strong face with the quiet smile will not be forgotten. Nor will Genny. She is back in Kushiro, serving again as a missionary in the city where she and Ralph had served together.

October 12

This evening as Doris and I were sitting in our kitchen-dining room, the building shook, the windows rattled, the lamp swayed, and the little short-wave radio on the table trembled and teetered. In a few seconds it was over. We looked at each other and smiled. It was just another minor earthquake. In the course of a year Japan has hundreds of such little tremors.

October 14

After a morning rain the skies cleared at noon. I left Kushiro just after 12:00 and rode west on the 26-kilometer bike trail. In the open country I found myself surrounded by beauty. I saw cloud shadows on the forested ridges, emerald-green fields, and sunlight on the autumn leaves.

At kilometer 18 I became aware that my rear tire was rubbing against a projecting bolt. In fact, the bolt end was beginning to groove the tire, and a blowout was imminent. I needed a screwdriver to partially withdraw the bolt, but I had no tools, and there was no town anywhere nearby — not even a farmhouse. When in desperation I picked up a flattened tin can and tried to use it as a makeshift screwdriver, I only succeeded in scraping my left hand.

With much trepidation I rode two kilometers farther. Then just beyond a bend I saw off to my left a cluster of farm buildings. A lane led me to the barn and there I found the farmer and his ten- or eleven-year-old daughter working with hammer and saw on a building addition.

With eloquent sign language I indicated my problem. The farmer stopped his work, extracted the bolt, ground off the end with a power tool, and refitted it. When his alert daughter heard me say the word "American," she ran to the house and quickly returned with her geography book. She put it on the ground and turned the pages to a world map. I put my finger on the U.S. and then on northern Japan. "America, Hokkaido, Kushiro," I said. Again she ran to the house, apparently at her father's bidding, and brought back a pen and tablet. When I caught on that they wanted my name and address, I printed them with block letters. All this was done with gestures, smiles, and the barest minimum of vocabulary. Then the little girl was off to the house a third time. She had noticed blood on my hand. She came back with a band-aid, opened it, and tenderly put it in position. With many *arigatos* (thank-yous), bows, and smiles, I returned to the trail and again headed west.

After a few kilometers I met Mary Beyler, a Mennonite missionary serving in Kushiro, who was also on a bike hike. We returned to the dairy farm and with her assistance as interpreter I thanked my benefactors properly and also learned their names (Ikuo Shimizu and his daughter Miho).

Mary and I then rode back to Kushiro. Just before dark, in a field beside the bike trail, we saw a pair of red-crested cranes — tall, stately, black and white creatures. They regarded us with dignity.

October 16

Doris and I are impressed by Kaneko-san, the Nakashibetsu pastor. He is courteous, urbane, knowledgeable. His appearance is so distinguished that one could easily imagine him in the Diet (Congress, Parliament) in Tokyo. For four years he served at radio station HCJB, "the Voice of the Andes," in Quito, Ecuador. Now he is serving here. With spiritual vitality and efficiency, he and Chieko-san, his wife, are building a strong congregation.

October 19

I'm becoming aware of the pressure of the Japanese work-place. When a worker joins a firm a marriage occurs. The worker identifies with mind, heart, and soul — and not only for the six-day workweek, but on Sundays also when committee work, improvement seminars, and company-sponsored social activities can make additional demands on time.

Charles, my brother, recently wrote on this. "This

scourge of busyness was with us in Hokkaido, too, but it weighs much heavier on our work here in Tokyo. You want to visit someone. But when do you do it? If he or she works, they likely don't get home until 9 or 10 at night or even later. On weekends they finally have a little time for relaxation and family. Also, we're busy then at the church. So it's easy to give up home visitation (other than retired people or housewives on occasion).

"We want so badly to have a weekday Bible study or prayer meeting. We try it. Who comes? Who is able to come? Almost no one. How about an occasional youth meeting or a picnic on Sunday? Great idea! But young people, whether students or employees, have an endless round of obligatory activities, on campus or with fellow employees, that can only be done on Sundays. What about the cottage meeting approach in people's homes at their convenience? If they are working people, they have no convenience. So by and large, our house meetings are at our house or the homes of retired people.

"The more dedicated people will come a little early on Sunday mornings for a seekers' class or stay awhile after worship on Sunday afternoons for fellowship, and that is about the size of the local church program."

October 20

After the Bible class at Nakashibetsu, Ken Shenk, my nephew and interpreter, drove us to Kaiyodai, a high observation point about 12 miles to the northwest. We looked down over flat, fertile farmland in a great arc from the northeast to the southwest. And off to the east was the big Russian-held island of Kunashiri. Russia seized Kunashiri, Etorofu (still further to the east), the small islands just east of the Nemuro Peninsula, Shikotan Island, and the Juriles at the end of World War II. They are all referred to as "Russian-held," but they might as well be described as "Russian" for there seems no chance at all Russia will ever give them back.

So for the first time I was looking at Russia. But I

didn't feel like Moses on Pisgah; I didn't feel I was viewing the Promised Land. I was seeing an island outpost of a nation that, to us Americans, is oppressive to its own people and hostile to us — and, yes, hostile to the Christian faith as well.

Yet I am sure that to many or most Russians the United States is the chief threat to world peace, and I believe too that the majority of the Russian people want peace as intensely as the majority of Americans. In regard to future peace the chief problem I suspect is not the peoples of the two nations; it is their political and military leaders.

October 21

In our rented Nissan "Bluebird" Ken, Doris, and I drove from Nakashibetsu to the Notsuke Peninsula, a low, rocky, narrow arm of land that curves outward from the eastern coast of Hokkaido. From the beach we looked northward across ten miles of tossing dark water to the southwestern tip of Kunashiri. And 100 yards inland from the surf we saw evidence of the heavy storms that beat against this unprotected peninsula. Hunched over and half-flattened, the few bushes and trees all face the south. The savage north winds of winter have stunted and humbled them.

The only vocation here is fishing, and it abounds. While we watched, a fishing boat came in. With an attached cable, a heavy tractor pulled it from the sea onto a series of timbers to protect its keel from the stony beach. Then hundreds of big salmon, flipping and jerking, were flung by hand from the hold into a waiting truck. The tractor drove down the beach and into the ocean, scooped up hundreds of gallons of sea water in its big front maw, and dumped it into the truck. Then off sped the truck.

October 25

Today I left the Obihiro Bible School and walked toward an indoor swimming pool. Since it was nearly three miles away, I kept watching for a bus. Finally I saw one coming, dashed to the nearest bus stop, and waited. But even though I was waving vigorously, it went past me. Then it slowed and stopped — about 150 feet up the street. I girded up my loins and ran. When the door opened there stood a sweet young girl (about 16) with a big smile and a questioning *"Hai?"* (Yes?"). I looked beyond her and saw that the bus was full of little children. It was a kindergarten bus! A non-yellow one. I made my futile apologies in English and bowed and smiled, and the bus drove on.

October 27
This morning at the Obihiro Mennonite Church we sang "Beneath the Cross of Jesus." It was written in England by Elizabeth Clephane in 1869. In Japan that was the year of the Meiji Restoration, the drastic shift in political power and direction that ended Japan's 200 years of total isolation, and flung her for better or for worse into the embrace of the modern world. It came to me that this poem, this hymn, has probably been of greater importance to human beings than the Meiji Restoration itself.

October 31
Today Mary Beyler took us to an *ikebana* (flower arranging) display. In a great hall we saw hundreds of exhibits. It was like walking through an art gallery. I discovered that while there are different schools of this art form all ikebana artists agree that the arranging should be asymmetrical. Mary said, "When Japanese flower arrangers want to do a spoof on American arranging, they jam a lot of flowers into a vase and make sure that the outline of the blossoms is perfectly rounded. They think that is hilarious." Ikebana experts also agree that usually an arrangement should have high, low, and intermediate elements. Seemingly this is considered artistic, and apparently the three levels also symbolize the relationship

between the heavens, the earth, and the people between.

November 2

On October 21 after leaving the Notsuke Peninsula and driving up into the scenic Shiretoka region, Ken, Doris and I turned westward at the fishing village of Rausu and drove toward the top of Shiretoka Pass. Our highway swung in great curves as we ascended higher and higher.

Half a mile below the crest we stopped and looked back. Just below us was a profusion of stunted trees, bare now with winter only days away and strangely beautiful with their gnarled white branches. Further to the east and far below were scores of low hills and summits, and still further east lay the open sea and mountainous offshore Kunashiri. As I tried to take it all in, I felt a sudden sense of pain.

I have tried to understand this relationship between beauty and pain. Two factors were present, I believe. One was my frustration that I would never be able to fully describe the panorama below me. And the other was a sharp awareness of the transitoriness of life. Someday I must leave this natural splendor. While I believe in heaven, its towers are barely visible at the horizon of life and death. But trees and mountains and sea and sky are tangible, physical, compelling; I clutch at them.

November 5

On this clear, bright, and windy day I left our apartment at 12:30 and rode west on the bike trail. At first the city buildings protected me from the sweep of the wind, but once I was clear of the city the strong headwind almost brought me to a standstill. I was stubborn however and fought my way kilometer by kilometer into the open country. After stopping at kilometer 6 and resting for a few minutes in the lee of a small building, I pushed on westward.

Just east of the kilometer 8 marker shadows crossed me from left to right. I looked up, and directly overhead, not over 30 feet above me, were three red-crested cranes, great black and white birds against a deep blue sky. They were flying close together, their bodies angled against the buffeting wind, making their way to the northeast. "Oh, my God," I said. Not profanity. A prayer. I watched them until they were out of sight behind a stand of low trees in the marsh.

November 7

Since Doris must judge an English contest tomorrow in Nakashibetsu, I went alone by rail to Obihiro. My Japanese seatmate identified me as an American — we can't hide — and also noticed my Bible. He asked me a question (I could not handle his language but he had a partial capacity in mine, and so English became our medium). "How can you Christians come from America to Vietnam and fight and kill and then go back to your churches and pray?" Although his wording wasn't quite that coherent I got the point. I replied that not all those who call themselves Christian are Christians in fact, and that not all deeds by Christians are good deeds. It was only a partial answer of course to a complex question.

When I found he was from Sapporo, I asked if he knew any Christians there. But he misunderstood my question and thought I was asking if he wanted to become a Christian. He replied, "Perhaps when I am sick and lonely."

"You need Jesus now, and Jesus needs you," I said.

After I arrived in Obihiro and told Tanase-san the story, he said, "He sounds so Japanese." I would add, "And so American."

November 8

Soon after boarding the Obihiro-Kushiro train, I left my seat and walked to the last car. When I found the door at the far end unlocked I opened it and made my way via a narrow passageway to the rear power unit. (These trains have diesel engines at both front and rear. The "front" engine pulls the train east, and then the "rear" engine is activated and takes its turn for the trip west.) I then opened a final door and saw three steps going up to the deactivated control cabin. At the top of the stairs and on the right side of the cabin, a trainman was sitting, looking through the curved glass at the receding track. When I indicated with gestures that I wanted to sit in the left seat, he nodded approval. So I climbed up. After ten kilometers he got off at Ikeda and I was there alone.

Later I went forward and bought a box of potato chips. I returned then and sat in the engineer's seat, ate chips, and watched the scenery. The train ran slowly past small, green, isolated farms and between low, wooded ridges. East of Atsunai where the railroad closely parallels the coast, I saw big breakers coming in, spray flying high from their curling, foaming crests.

At 3:55 as we approached Kushiro it was nearly dark. Hokkaido lies far to the north and in late fall the night comes quickly.

November 10

At a conference a few days ago a Japanese woman spoke to the group about her religious experience. Ken served as a silent interpreter for Doris and me, writing rapidly and then passing the sheets to us. "It has been only a year and a half since I became a Christian. I came from a Christian family but resisted for a long time. As a teenager, I decided I was not meant to be a Christian. I had an idea that being a Christian means being perfect. I'm close to 40 now, so that means I've resisted the faith for 20 years. What a waste of my life! I used to say that it's okay if all I have is this life. When I talk about my journey, I can't help but weep. I have a human trait of not being able to quite believe, but I came to a place where I had to say that I needed God beside me. I was half crazy when I got to that stage. When I told God I needed Him by me, I literally felt light even though I was in a dark room. God answered me with this strange experience of light within darkness."

So it was with Augustine. He too came to Christ when he was approaching mid-life, and he too was touched by light in the moment of conversion.

November 12

Today a card in Japanese came from Miho Shimizu, the fifth-grader who lives near kilometer 20 on the bike trail and who with her father helped me four weeks ago. Genny and Shirasaka-san (and later Mary) worked on the translation. It goes like this: "Dear uncle, Thank you for the very beautiful picture postcard. Is your finger healed? What time did you return home that day? Please come and visit again. Miho Shimizu." Shirasaka-san says Miho means "beautiful young sprout" and Shimizu means "pure water." All Japanese names have meanings.

November 13

Recently a friend loaned us a series of clippings from the "Asahi Shimbun," an English newspaper. One is entitled, "Japan is a Rich Country Filled with People Who Live Poorly." The opening sentence: "Japan is a wealthy nation whose citizens do not enjoy many of the amenities of wealth." An illustration is given of the Shihiko Sugimoto family. Is this a fictitious name? Probably. The house "would be Spartan by American standards. . . . By Japanese standards, it borders on the luxurious. . . . Mrs. Sugimoto has no sewers, no central heating, no dishwasher, no clothes dryer." Yet her house, 90 minutes from downtown Tokyo, is in a fine neighborhood. Houses sell for about $250,000, and many of the neighbors drive Mercedes autos. The Sugimoto home does have color TV, a stereo, and a video cassette recorder. "After the lack of sewers, Mrs. Sugimoto and her friends believe the toughest problem facing the Japanese is the expense of land and the resulting crowded housing. The problem is particularly acute in Tokyo, which has the best jobs and the least space." The Sugimoto home has two small bedrooms downstairs and three upstairs (two of which are rented out), a kitchen with a small table, a tiny study for the husband, and a 9 x 12 combination family and living room. The wife cooks on a two-burner portable range. "To get hot water, the Sugimotos must first turn on gas water heaters, one for the kitchen and one for the *ofuro*, the deep Japanese bath. . . .

November 15

I discovered yesterday that in order to get extensions for our three-month visas we must first apply for alien registration status. Then this morning I was told that the registration is just a formality — apart from the indignity of being fingerprinted.

In the afternoon Doris and I went to the municipal building and were formally registered as aliens. I am an alien. Doris is an alien. It gives me a new feeling for the Children of Israel in Egypt and for our spiritual pilgrimage in 1985. But we were not fingerprinted! I was prepared to accept it, though under protest.

November 18

The Amish of America are much admired here. The Japanese respect their group solidarity, self-discipline, capacity for hard work, willingness and ability to "take care of their own," and respect for ecology. All of these qualities of course are quite "Japanese."

November 19

Wherever I see Japanese workers I see things happening. Recently while returning by train from Obihiro, I was sitting in the rear power unit looking back at the roadbed. The train slowed to a crawl at several points as it moved past waiting track-and-tie repairmen, and each time, as soon as the rear unit had gone by, the men immediately sprang back onto the roadbed. Within seconds they were again at work.

In the U.S. a leisurely return to the tracks might take

five or ten minutes. In Central America it might take an hour.

November 20
When I got up at 8:00 our rooms were cold. In the bathroom I saw my breath. As is common in Japan we have no central heating; we have only a kerosene stove. It cannot be regulated to keep room heat at a desired level, and so we turn it on when the room is cold and then turn it off when the room gets hot. It's Siberia or the Sahara.

For safety we shut off the stove at night, and in the morning it's an act of courage to crawl out of bed and turn it on. Sometimes Doris does it; sometimes I do. Our stove is a slow starter. After the initial buttons are pushed, five minutes must elapse before it "clicks" — and only then does the heat even begin to come. With the sliding doors to the "den" and the entranceway closed, our main room finally gets warm within 90 minutes. Meanwhile we cope by inhabiting the area near the stove and donning layers of clothing.

November 21
I have tried to discover why the Christian Church in Japan has grown so slowly. Of course it must be said that there was a time when it grew rapidly. From the arrival of Francis Xavier in 1549 until the outbreak of persecution (1597) and the subsequent retreat of Japan into isolation, the Roman Catholic Church flourished. At one point there were at least 300,000 Christians, and there may have been a half-million.

Then a dramatic reversal occurred. Christianity was prohibited, frightful persecutions were launched, the Christian Church went underground to survive, and Japan closed all doors against foreign culture, commerce, and religion. The doors remained shut for over 200 years.

When this era of total isolation and anti-Christian laws ended soon after Commodore Perry's 1853 naval visit, about 20,000 *kakure kirishtan* ("hidden Christians") emerged from a seven-generation ordeal. Most of these staunch individuals affiliated with the modern Roman Catholic Church. They were joined in the task of expanding the faith by a large band of Protestant missionaries. In spite of great efforts since then by both wings of Christianity, membership in Japan today is only 1,120,000 — less than one percent of the population. By contrast, nearly a quarter of the people in nearby South Korea are considered to be Christian.

Why the slow growth in Japan? I have pestered friends on this and they have struggled to give me answers. They struggle because it's a complex thing and even Christian scholars don't fully agree.

The answers I hear most often are these: (1) the centuries-old influence of Shinto, Buddhism, and Confucianism in binding the individual into a unique and rigid society; (2) the Japanese tendency to oppose or at least question foreign ideas, and the identification of Christianity as a "foreign" religion; (3) the lack of any basis in traditional Japanese thought for the concept of a personal, all-powerful God; (4) the distrust in Japan of organized religion (in recent centuries both Shinto and Buddhism were in close alliance with oppressive regimes); (5) the offense produced in many Japanese minds by the exclusive claims of Christianity; and (6) the clash between the concept of a God who is over the nations — and the nation-centered ethic of Japan.

November 22

Last night at Obihiro Bible School an interpretation problem arose during the class. Takio Tanase, always knowledgeable and precise, was my interpreter. I was speaking of the Book of the Law — its discovery and the dramatic consequences in II Kings 22 — and said, "It was probably Deuteronomy 28 (with all its curses) in the Book of the Law that scared the liver out of King Josiah." The usually unflappable Tanase-san staggered at the liver-fright allusion but then found a way to say it in

Japanese.

Ten days ago I threw a curve at my nephew Ken who has been my excellent interpreter for sermons and Bible lectures in congregations. During the Sunday morning service at Bekkai I was speaking on Acts 10:36 and talking about "the good news of peace." I was not aware that Ken was translating this, and correctly so, as "the gospel of peace." Then when I said, "The good news is the gospel," Ken waggled his head as if to say, "How do I handle this?" I was asking him to say, "The gospel is the gospel." He was resourceful however and found a new route through the verbal thicket.

In September Charles told of an American preacher who arrived in Tokyo and with his interpreter began his first sermon. He led off with a detailed illustration that was replete with Americanisms, puns, and plays on words. At the end of three minutes he paused and turned expectantly to his interpreter. The good gentleman faced the audience and said in Japanese, "It is absolutely impossible to translate that story. Just go ahead and laugh." The audience did so, and much encouraged, the speaker plunged into his next point.

November 23

A man on the train asked me, "What do you think of Japan?" Rather directly — I think too directly — I gave him several pro and con answers. "I like the natural beauty and the sensitivity of the people to beauty. I like the little children, the hard work I see, and the fact that there is little street crime. I don't like the way Japan treats its Korean 'aliens' who live here, and I don't like the word *gaijin*. I also think there is too much hard work."

I could also have said that I like the neatness and order, the group loyalties, and the graciousness to tourists-in-need. And I could have said that I don't like the heavy hand of tradition, the lack of warmth in many marriages, the lack of absolute moral standards in Shinto and Buddhism, the tendency to denigrate women, and certain

over-rigid patterns (for example, the severe dress regulations for high school students).

November 25

Nearly all Japanese people have a loose affiliation with
both Shinto and the Japanese form of Buddhism. Shinto
is oriented to nature and also to the nation. While Shinto
adherents worship the spirits who dwell in the visible
forms of nature (rocks, trees, etc.), they also think of
Shinto as the unique religion of Japanese nationalism.
Buddhism is oriented to enlightenment and existence
after death. In a very simplified way, we may say that
Shinto enrolls the newly-born into the cult of the state,
and that Buddhism formally enrolls the deceased into the
realm of death. The two religions are supplementary;
they almost constitute a single religion. Japanese don't
think of themselves as being devotees of the one as compared to the other. Another element in Japanese religion
is Confucianism with its emphases of obedience to social
norms and respect for superiors.

November 26

Last night Doris and I stayed at the home of Yaguchi-
san, pastor of the Shalom church in Sapporo, and
Mitsuko-san, his second wife. Reiko-san, his first wife,
died in 1970.

In addition to serving as a pastor, Yaguchi-san teaches
English at a Sapporo university, espouses Japanese peace
concerns, writes poetry (thus far he has eight published
volumes), and is interested in church planting. He wants
to help establish congregations in southwestern Hokkaido, and then he would like the church to leap the
Tsugaru Strait to the main island of Honshu. "We might
hear a Macedonian call," he said.

Yaguchi has two sons, Yobu (Job) and Yujin (Eugene).
Yobu is a student at Goshen Biblical Seminary, Elkhart,
Indiana, and Yujin is a university freshman in Sapporo.
Within one or two years Yujin may be at Goshen College.

Yujin has a reputation for self-reliance. Once when he was seven, he became separated from his parents in the cavernous Sapporo City Hall. After he was reunited with his family, someone asked him if he had been scared. "No," he replied, "I would have been if I had been lost. But I wasn't lost; you were."

November 29
Large numbers of Japanese people try valiantly, and with much success, to master English. At one particular point however Japanese students of English have difficulty in pronunciation. Due to their own phonetic patterns they find it almost impossible to distinguish between the English "l" and "r" sounds. One of our hostesses in Sapporo last weekend — a gracious, vivacious person with excellent English — was concerned about the long walk I was about to take through unfamiliar terrain, and said to me as I left, "Good ruck!" And a skilled English teacher recently spoke to me about a "Reica" camera. One more. A sign in the Kushiro rail station points helpfully to the *RAVATOLY*.

But I can scarcely use Japanese at all. Moreover, I cannot pronounce properly the "r" in "Kushiro." Recently I said it six or eight times after Ken and Genny, and each time I thought I was pronouncing it exactly as they did, but I never got it right. A certain flip of the tongue-tip against the roof of the mouth escaped me.

December 2
In today's "Yomiuri," a daily English newspaper, is a review by Jorge Ribeiro of the book *Hiroshima Maidens* by Rodney Barker. It's about the 25 Hiroshima women who had been disfigured by the A-Bomb and who finally received plastic surgery in the United States.

The review says that the 25 women were at a U.S. air base in Japan and had already boarded the military transport which was to take them to New York City for their surgery — when suddenly a U.S. State Department cable arrived with word that the flight was cancelled. Someone in Washington, possibly fearing bad publicity for the United States, had become nervous about the project.

General John Hull, the officer in charge at the base, read the cable "with dismay. . . .For a long minute the general said nothing. Then, with a heavy sigh, he handed the cable back to his aide. 'Unfortunately I don't have my reading glasses with me,' he said. 'Be sure to remind me to read this later.'" The plane took off on schedule. Marvelous. If that was a lie, I think God smiled. And the angels laughed.

December 3

Mimoto-san, the splendid Kushiro pastor, and his wife Chisako-san took us today to Bihoro Pass and Lake Kussharo. On the eastern shore of Kussharo we saw many Siberian swans. These magnificent birds fly east from Siberia each November to winter in Hokkaido, and many stay at this lake because of warm springs at the water's edge.

As we stood at the lakeside three started takeoff runs. With powerful wing-beats and threshing legs they lifted their heavy bodies a few inches above the water and there they flew almost interminably, seemingly unable to rise further, their wings flailing and their feet taking long strides on the smooth surface of the lake. Then ponderously, like overloaded 747s, they rose skyward in long gentle arcs.

December 7

It gets colder and colder. That is true in the Hokkaido hinterland, and it's true inside our apartment. Actually the outside temperature last night was no lower that 12 degrees Fahrenheit. At home with our well-insulated house and central heating that would be no problem.

Although Japan has many modern houses and more are under construction, especially in big cities, large numbers of traditional houses (non-insulated and without central heating) are still being built. Why? Cost factors, of course, are part of the answer. It's also a matter of tradition. Most people here don't really expect to stay warm in winter. Instead, they exhort themselves and others with *"gaman! gaman!"* ("bear it! bear it!").

December 8

I keep thinking of a statement by Mary Beyler at a recent conference. "I have a number of friends who say, 'I don't have time to be a Christian. Maybe later in life. But now I can't give up my Sundays.'" The super-loyalty required by employers preempts nearly all free time and makes Christian Sunday observance difficult.

December 11

Never have I lived in a country where so much beautiful food turns out to be tasteless, mealy, soggy, or dough-like. But I'm getting carried away. After all, I have written to U.S. friends, "All the food is beautiful and some of it is tasty." I try to enjoy the food. I want to be a good guest — and all the more so because our hostesses are models of graciousness.

December 12

This evening at Mimoto-san's, Doris and I received a marvelous gift, a large (11" by 15") hand-wrought 1986 calendar. On the cover page is the title, "Calendar of Paper Folding," and below are the words "By Yumiko and Chisako Mimoto." In addition to the cover it has six heavy-paper pages. Each of the six contains two months of the year, with each month symbolized by decorations in the *origami* (paper-folding) Japanese art form.

For Doris and me it is totally unique. We keep looking at the symbols for the different months — for example, plum blossoms and the nightingale for February, tulips for April, chrysanthemums for November, and Jesus and cattle for December.

December 16

On this brilliantly clear morning we flew from Kushiro to Tokyo. Ten minutes after take-off we saw the long sweep of the jagged, impressive range west of Obihiro. Its lower slopes and higher rock faces and battlements were superb in their winter dress.

Over northern Honshu I looked down on a geometric fantasy of sharp-angled mountain surfaces — on tilted planes of virgin snow and wind-scoured black rock. Further south the sun was shining on innumerable winter rice fields. They looked like spun silk in neat rectangles or like silver-tinted *tatami* mats.

December 17

When I woke early this morning I looked out the window, and there was snow-clad Fuji, glowing pink in the first rays of the sun.

Later I went downtown to the Ginza and saw red and green Christmas decorations in profusion. Strings of colored lights covered building fronts, and display windows featured Santas, reindeer, evergreens, and miniature winter landscapes. The Japanese have adopted Christmas, or at least its trappings, with enthusiasm. Three weeks ago Tanase-san told me of a Japanese man on the Ginza at Christmas-time who saw a group of Christians decorating their church. He asked with astonishment, "Do you Christians celebrate Christmas too?"

December 18

In Japan people speak of going "up to Tokyo." You go "up to Tokyo" in terms of vocation, education, prestige, and wealth. When you leave, you go "down from Tokyo." The term is similar to the Biblical "up to Jerusalem," except that Jerusalem is literally high and Tokyo is practically at sea level on the Kanto Plain.

Today we went "down from Tokyo." We took the Shinkansen (bullet-train) north to Morioka — 330 miles in two hours and 45 minutes. The speedometer needle in the dining car rode past the 210 kilometer per hour mark (130 mph). Rice fields and irrigation canals flashed by. Northbound autos on parallel roads were quickly overtaken and left behind. They didn't quite look as if they were moving backward — but almost. We ran in and out of tunnels. Some of them were only two or three seconds from portal to portal. Since Shinkansen speeds require level track, even low insignificant hills are pierced.

At Morioka in the early afternoon we exchanged our shining Pegasus of the rails for a plodding old railroad workhorse. It carried us up into the mountains to the west. Deep snow. Tunnels, trestles, snow-laden evergreens. Ice-crusted mountainsides that gleamed silver in the afternoon sun. This area (northwestern Honshu, just east of the Sea of Japan) is part of Japan's "snow country." We emerged from the mountains in late afternoon and came down to snowy Akita on the seacoast.

In our Akita hotel room I perused with fascination the "Regulations" book. Among its items: "Guests are not allowed to bring under mentioned articles in passage or room.

    a. animals and/or birds

    b. extremely bad-smelling articles

    c. extremely large quantity luggages

    d. catch fire easily or inflammable articles such as gunpowder or volatile oil

    e. guns or swords not allowed to possess legally by authority"

Also: "Guests are not allowed to trouble others by singing with a loud voice. . . .It is prohibited to play gambles and or injure public moralities. . . .Please refrain from cast articles away from a window." The next regulation carried a note of mystery but sounded interesting. "Please refrain from going to restaurant, bar, coffee shop, or outside with *Yukata*." Who or what is "*Yukata*?" A waitress? A chambermaid? I learned much later that "*Yukata*" is the bathrobe placed in each room for the convenience of guests. So much for my vivid imagination.

December 19

For long distances our route southward from Akita lay along the Sea of Japan. Rocky promontories at the crescent-tips of little curving bays. Big grey combers coming in. Snow-covered villages with houses huddled together between the sea and the hills. High rocks in the surf and offshore, their foundations in the foam, and with trees growing from their unpromising summits. Cove after cove with black boulders and white surf and with heavy spray-fog hanging in the air.

In the afternoon we went southeast from Niigata to Tokyo on another leg of the Shinkansen system. We saw Fuji clearly just before entering the far-flung outskirts of Tokyo, but then lost it in the haze and smoke of Greater Tokyo.

December 20

Today we rode the bullet-train to Hiroshima. Four hours and thirty-five minutes, including stops. 895 kilometers (556 miles). We came into Hiroshima just at sunset. As we ran through the final tunnel in the encircling hills, I said to myself, What will I think here?

After we were settled in our room at the World Friendship Center, I left for a two-mile walk to the center of the city, to the T-shaped bridge over the Aioi River, the bombardier's aiming point. It was a cool night with a light rain falling.

I found my way to the Motayasu River — and on to the ruined, softly-lighted A-Bomb dome. I walked a few hundred feet further and out onto the Aioi Bridge. What can I say? I have read Hersey's *Hiroshima* and Dryden's *Day One*. But how can one imagine the suddenly expanding, incandescent fireball, the shock wave, the searing heat, the flame, the thunder, the silence — and then the cries?

December 21

In the Peace Memorial Museum we saw a stone flower holder that had stood 370 meters from the hypocenter, the point directly beneath the midair burst. On one side it is scarred and whitened. Nearby we saw a short flight of stone steps that once stood at the entrance to a building — and only a short distance from the hypocenter. A human shadow is imprinted on the stone. The heat-light from the blast overhead scoured shades lighter the stone surfaces that were not "protected" by the human body. The result: a dark shadow on the stone, the shadow of a human being. And what of the human being? Instant fiery dissolution. Disappearance.

Four days from now we will celebrate Christmas. What aeons and nebulae of contrast endlessly extend between the Bethlehem event and the Hiroshima event, between the Babe and the Bomb. The Bethlehem night was holy. "O Holy Night," we sing. But what can one sing at Hiroshima? What elegy or funeral chant could ever mount up to do justice to the theme?

December 24

By prearrangement we met Charles and Ruth yesterday at 11:00 a.m. on the Hiroshima rail platform. They were standing beside the coach door of the bullet-train that had brought them from Tokyo. We all boarded quickly (the train stopped only two minutes) and rode together to Hakata — and then, after a train change, on to Nagasaki.

With its narrow harbor entrance, encompassing mountains, and new buildings, Nagasaki is a splendid city. It is also somewhat forgotten. Everyone knows about the Hiroshima A-Bomb of August 6, 1945, but few remember that a second one was dropped on Nagasaki three days later. Nor is its Christian history widely known or remembered. Nagasaki was the first great Christian center in Japan. It was here especially that in the 16th century the Roman Catholic Church took root and flourished mightily — before the coming of massive persecution.

Today we went to the rebuilt Urakami Church, the successor to the one destroyed August 9, 1945. There are ghosts and terrible memories here. Of the parish membership of 12,000 only 3,500 survived the Bomb. The ghosts began to take visible form as I stood in the garden at the front of the church and looked at statues of saints, their stone garments scarred and blistered, facing the epicenter as they did on the day of holocaust. Nearby two statues stand headless.

December 25

Charles, Ruth, Doris and I traveled today in our Hertz car to the Sotome countryside, northwest of Nagasaki. In this area many Christians suffered martyrdom in the 17th century and others went underground. We wanted to learn more about them.

In a small museum we found a document from the early 1600s on persecutions. Charles and Ruth stood in front of the glass case and worked together at translating it. "They were persecuted. They received almost more than they could bear, but rather than relinquish their faith, they sacrificed their precious lives to God and in the midst of the flames sang hymns of praise. Through the singing of songs their faith supported them through the terrible suffering of martyrdom." It reads like Hebrews 11 and like *Fox's Book of Martyrs* and *The Martyrs' Mirror*. One persecution date mentioned in the museum is 1614, the year that Hans Landis, the last Anabaptist martyr of Switzerland, was beheaded.

As the 17th century persecutions expanded in fury and terror, clusters of Christians in this Sotome area founded a secret Church that passed on the faith for seven generations. These were the *kakure kirishtan* (the "hidden Christians"). In 1865 when Japan was beginning to open, a group of them came to the Oura Church in Nagasaki and proclaimed, "We are of the same faith as you." The "hidden Christians" had begun to emerge.

At Kurosaki we visited a large parish church of over 900 members, nearly all of them descended from the secret Christians who so determinedly kept the faith for centuries.

December 27

This morning we went to Nara. It was a cold day and a cold train, but Nara was worth it. The vast park has many Shinto shrines, Buddhist temples, and hundreds of tame deer.

Shinto structures are typically left with a natural wood finish; Buddhist temples often emphasize a red coloration. Shinto shrines are dedicated to a variety of objects. We saw a shrine dedicated to rice spoons. Yes, rice spoons. There is a "spirit" in them, too, just as in needles, dolls, rocks, trees, foxes, fire, waterfalls — in almost everything, it seems. This indicates the animistic basis of Shinto. Before leaving the Nara religious precincts we saw the Five-Story Pagoda of Kofkuji Temple. Then we visited the nearby American shrine of McDonald's.

December 28

We're staying tonight at the Anabaptist Center in the Honan-cho sector of Tokyo. While taking a 10:00 p.m. walk on the streets, I saw three men marching slowly and with measured step, almost as though on parade. One was carrying a lantern; the other two were striking together heavy, polished pieces of wood in a slow insistent rhythm. Intrigued, I followed them for blocks. What was the meaning of their solemn march? Back at the Center I asked Fritz Sprunger. "Oh," he said, "they're community-minded volunteers; they're warning people about fire danger ('Turn off your kerosene stoves, now that it's bedtime')."

This is our last night in Japan. Tomorrow we fly to Hong Kong.

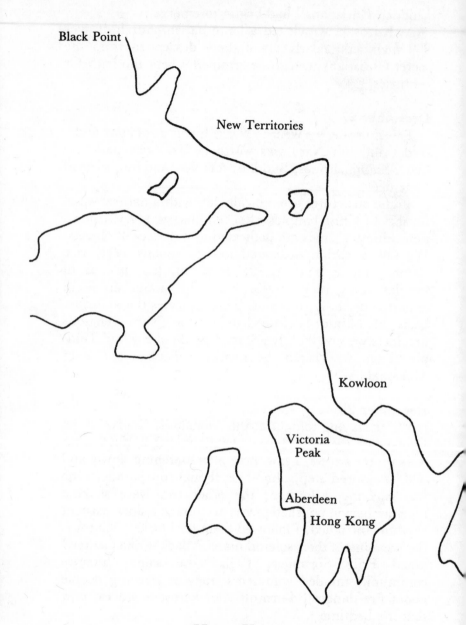

Hong Kong

Six Days
In Hong Kong

For years I have encountered stunning photographs of this Oriental skyscraper city and its teeming harbor, and I have read of its color and complexity at the gateway to a more drab and simplistic Communist China.

When it became clear that our mission journey from Tokyo to Pune, India, would route us via Hong Kong, I said to Doris, "Let's stop there for several days." She agreed, and it was quickly arranged.

We stayed at the "English Y" on Salisbury Street, walked the streets, rode the ferries, took tours, and shopped. And one day we went inland to Canton (Guangzhou).

December 29

I called Nagasaki "splendid," but for Hong Kong the word is "spectacular." Through rents in the clouds we caught our first glimpses of it as we entered the landing pattern. We saw steep green slopes, modern high rises, and the constricted busy waterway that is Victoria Harbor.

Our room at the "Y" on Salisbury Road is close to the waterfront and the Star ferry, and only two blocks from Nathan Road, the main north-south Kowloon thoroughfare. From the rooftop terrace, the view across the harbor at twilight is astonishing — the brilliantly lit skyscrapers of Hong Kong Island (festooned now with Christmas lights), and beyond and above them, the dark loom of the ridge against the still-bright evening sky. Manhattan from the Staten Island ferry or Weehauken barely compares.

December 30

Today we attended the Monday noon Mennonite fellowship in Kowloon. Two congregations, both sponsored by the Eastern Mennonite Board of Missions and using Cantonese and English, are here in this Far Eastern city. While Hong Kong may seem an improbable location for Mennonite missions, we seem to be putting roots down everywhere.

During our long walk back to the "Y" we saw high buildings (usually with shops, department stores, and theaters below — and apartments above), colorful billboards, modern window displays and wares, executive types with attaché cases, well-dressed women, crowded sidewalks, and bustle and activity. Everything in Kowloon seems to be close together and everyone is in a hurry.

In the evening we took the Star ferry for the ten-minute harbor crossing. Like the Staten Island ferry it is virtually an institution. Both have great skyline vistas across water, and both are amazingly economical. The Star ride is only 70 cents (Hong Kong), less than a U.S. dime.

December 31
Just thirty minutes before midnight I went for a short walk — if it could be called that. I couldn't make much progress. The sidewalks were jammed with New Year celebrants. It was like Times Square on New Year's Eve. When I came back a security man downstairs told me that Hong Kong observes the New Year twice — the English one on January 1 and the Chinese one a few weeks later.

January 1, 1986
During our bus tour today around Hong Kong Island we visited the Tanka boat community at Aberdeen. These are not new arrivals from war-ravaged Vietnam and Cambodia, but fisherfolk who have been here for generations. In a narrow curving inlet from the sea about 6,000 of them live on their multitudinous boats — sampans, scows, barges, floating restaurants and shops, floating temples, and hulks of every age and description. The sea-dwellers make their way from one boat to another by precarious little planks and walkways. Our guide told us that they consider it bad luck to set foot on land and so live out their entire lives on boats. I suspect he was pulling our legs a bit.

In a water taxi we took a 30-minute trip through the boat community. Back and forth we went in the narrow sea-lanes that bisect the sea-city. Many other taxis were also in use and the sun-bright water was choppy and heaving from their wakes. We saw women hanging up wash and scrubbing their decks — and from their boat domains "sea dogs" barked vigorously at us.

We arrived in mid-afternoon at a saddle on the high ridge near Victoria Peak. There we had a superb view of the city. Steep green mountains to right and left framed the central scene. Below us were commercial pinnacles —

and just beyond, scores of dark boats and white curving wakes on the blue harbor surface. On the other side of the harbor were the high, squarish, huddled buildings of Kowloon (space is at a premium and the buildings go high because there is nowhere else to go). Still further to the west and northwest lay the green and brown hills of the New Territories that front China itself.

January 3

This was our China day. In the morning we traveled by hovercraft to Canton (Guangzhou) and in the evening returned by train. I discovered that whereas a hydrofoil rides high on its fins, a hovercraft rides on a thin cushion of air. Except for the frequent occasions when our big 250-passenger craft slowed to avoid swamping smaller vessels with its bow wave, we cruised at about 30 miles an hour. Our route took us past Black Point at the southwestern tip of the New Territories and then into one of the mouths of the Pearl River. We saw ancient little fishing boats, each with its precarious thatched shelter at one end. And as we neared Canton we passed dozens of anchored freighters, all apparently waiting for dock space or for the ministrations of the swarming little lighters.

After our 12:40 p.m. arrival, we were taken through an unprepossessing customs building and then via a Nissan bus to a restaurant. On the way our guide told us that the population of Canton is four million and that the city has two million bicycles. (During the next seven hours I think we saw half of those bicycles.) The Mandarin dialect, he said, is now mandated. It has only four tones whereas Cantonese has nine. It occurred to me that a tone-deaf person would have a terrible time even with Mandarin. He also told us there are now three kinds of ownership: "government, collective, private." We passed a number of "free market" street stalls or tables where farmers and entrepreneurs were selling excess produce and miscellany. Our meal had eleven courses, most of them quite tasty.

Our first stop after lunch was the palatial home of the Chen family. It is now government property; the family fled in the late 40s. At a souvenir table we bought eleven little stone turtles, one for each of the grandchildren. In China, we were told, the turtle symbolizes long life. Then we went to the Dr. Sun Yat-sen Memorial Hall. While it is big — it seats 3,000 — its interior is colorless, drab, depressing. Our guide spoke of Sun Yat-sen as the "forerunner of the Democratic Revolution." I said, "Maybe Dr. Sun Yat-sen would be surprised if he knew what kind of revolution he started." Since I got no real response, I pressed the point. "Maybe he didn't know he was starting a Marxist Revolution."

"Oh, yes," the guide replied quickly. "Maybe he didn't know that."

After additional tour stops and a snack at the modern China Hotel, we went to the train station. Even though it was already dark when our train pulled out, I was able to see hovels and garden plots beside the right-of-way, seedy-looking high apartment buildings, and masses of bicycles at road crossings. Further out in the rural area I could make out small neat fields, many of them carefully ridged, and some with straight green rows of vegetables. I also saw irrigation canals and channels.

The word for today was gray. This was the predominant impression. Yes, the sky was overcast and a gray pall of haze shrouded much of what we saw, and I can't blame China for that. But we saw grayness and drabness at a multitude of places — in the villages and buildings along the river and in Canton itself. What a contrast it all was with the vivid slashes of color one encounters everywhere in Hong Kong.

Now I know all about Mainland China; I was there seven hours. Which book shall I write first?

January 4

At the McDonald's where we went for a late breakfast

the decor featured large plaques of a number of the States (Maryland, Virginia...). To our amusement we found we had sat down with our trays just beneath the Indiana design. Our home state! "Back home again in Indiana."

In today's "South China Morning Post" the weather forecast says, "It will be sunny during the day with a maximum temperature of about 16 degrees." That is a Celsius figure; in Fahrenheit it is about 61 degrees. The forecast then adds, "Continuing cold tomorrow." "Cold?" Good grief! After our Hokkaido December we are in a state of bliss.

This afternoon we sauntered through several ivory shops, looking in vain for a salt and pepper set. We did spot an amazing variety of explicit erotic pieces. We also saw a fabulous pleasure boat of the type once enjoyed by Oriental potentates. It was large, detailed, and exquisite — completely carved from ivory. We could have bought it for only 400,000 Hong Kong dollars (about 60,000 U.S.). "Ten percent off for cash?" I asked the girl behind the counter.

"Yes," she said with a smile.

Late in the evening Doris and I took a final trip on the Star ferry. On the mountains west of the city we saw spreading patterns and perimeters of forest fires. Little rain has fallen for weeks and the trees and brush on the mountain slopes are extremely dry.

January 5

On this Sunday morning we went to a religious fellowship on the 17th floor of the Ambassador Hotel. The Church Directory at the "Y" had referred to it as a "Brethren" congregation. And a Brethren service it was, and we enjoyed it and gladly participated in the worship, even though it was not in the German Pietist and Alexander Mack tradition we had expected.

No pastor was in evidence, but four or five members rose as if on cue and ministered from the Word. Hymns were sung and the Lord's Supper observed. Quite obviously the group was Biblically oriented and conservative in theology and piety. A quick perusal of the bulletin indicated that the Ambassador Fellowship, its official name, is active in education, medical work, church planting, and youth work.

Who were these good people? I am sure they were Plymouth Brethren, so named because Plymouth, England, was one of their major 19th century points of origin. Oh, yes, at the end of the service I found that many of the local members had English and Scottish origins.

It was good to be there, but my eye kept straying to the nearby window and to the vista far below of the busy boats in Victoria Harbor.

In the afternoon we flew to Bangkok — 1200 miles across the South China Sea, Vietnam, and Laos. According to the flight plan we crossed the Vietnam coastline near Hue. Actually, the coast was covered by clouds, but soon afterward we flew into clear air and I saw a jungle river and mountains. A few minutes later the captain announced on the intercom that we were over the Mekong River and that visibility was unusually good. I checked the view on both sides of the plane and saw perhaps a hundred-mile stretch of it. Vietnam, Hue, Mekong. What poignant names! From 30,000 feet I could see so little of it, but if I had been walking or driving there, I might have seen more than I wanted.

We landed at Bangkok in late afternoon and then took a minibus to the Christian Guest House in the downtown area. On the way we saw a number of Japanese firm names: Toshiba, Isuzu, Hitachi, and Sogo. We also saw some American ones: Esso, Shell, Dairy Queen, A&W, and the ubiquitous McDonald's.

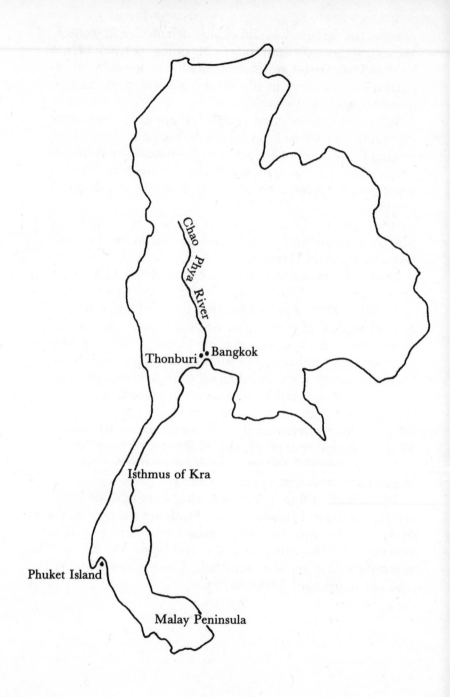

Thailand

Seven Days
In Bangkok

Our big task in Bangkok was to secure visas for India. In Japan we had been balked on this at every turn. Our applications hadn't been refused, but they hadn't been accepted either. We decided therefore to go on to Bangkok via Hong Kong and make a completely new start on the application process. For this we allotted seven days, and arranged our Hong Kong-Bangkok and Bangkok-Bombay flight reservations accordingly.

To our great surprise we received our visas on the first day after we arrived. Then we tried to move our flight schedule forward. At the seminary in India classes had already begun. My students were waiting. All flights to Bombay however were fully booked; we wouldn't be able to leave for six days. We were stranded in Bangkok. But what a marvelous place to be stranded! With sighs and grins we decided to make the best of it.

January 6

The people at the India Consulate were most gracious; they received our applications soon after 9:00 a.m. and told us we could pick up our visas at 4:00 p.m. And we did. It was almost too good to be true.

The Bangkok Christian Guest House is a splendid oasis. When we step out of our comfortable room we see green grass and flowering trees, even though all around us are the high buildings and the muffled roar of this Oriental metropolis. The meals are good and the management is efficient. In this Christian setting moreover we can meet other mission people, most of them here for a few days on business, or for a rest, or like ourselves while waiting for flights.

January 7

This was a day of details. I went to the American Express office to replenish our money supply and then to the Siam Travel Agency to plan post-India flights and apply for Burma visas. On our way from India to Singapore we will work for a week in Rangoon with a struggling Christian fellowship. After writing reports and letters we walked in the pleasant night air.

January 8

Today we took an eight-hour tour through the Thai countryside southwest of Bangkok. Even though in this region January is considered "cold," the weather is a delight to us. On this sunny day with a Fahrenheit temperature of 65 or 70, we saw much lush tropical terrain and fields of rice, sugar cane, and bananas.

As we were watching a modest industrial process (sugar extraction from coconuts) at a small roadside factory and tourist stop, a saleswoman approached Doris and held up a Thai wraparound skirt. It was a quality item. The price was 300 baht ($12 U.S.). "200," Doris said.

"280," countered the woman.

Doris got it for 200. Later, on the bus, a woman across

the aisle said it had been offered to her for 150!

At a village in the canal country west of Bangkok we enjoyed the floating market. This is a waterborne culture. Houses and shops are along canals, not highways. The car gives way to the boat. We stood beside a canal and watched a multitude of little market boats, each with its colorful cargo of fruits, vegetables, or flowers glide slowly past. Women in bright-colored blouses and slacks and with intricately woven wide-brimmed hats expertly wielded their paddles and maneuvered their craft amid the boat traffic.

In the pavilion at the Rose Gardens we saw Thai folk dances and enjoyed their grace, beauty, and precision. I liked especially the rhythms and adroit steps of the Mizo Bamboo Dance. Long poles of bamboo form a grid just above the floor level and are brought together, separated, and brought together again in a clacking rhythm that moves faster and faster. To avoid bruised or broken ankles great poise and agility are essential.

On the return trip to the city our minibus driver held his own with a vengeance amid the rapidly flowing streams of cars, buses, trucks, and three-wheelers. Bangkok has two kinds of pedestrians: the quick and the dead.

January 9

After taking a water taxi up the Chao Phya River, we got off at boat landing 8 and walked through the golden glitter of the Grand Palace. I have never seen such copious, extravagant usage of gold leaf. Within the palace precincts are scores of gleaming pagodas, chapels, and spires. It is architectural opulence. By moonlight it would be stunning.

On the interior surfaces of the enclosing walls are many hundreds of meters of historical and religious murals. They depict war, women, worship, and worldly vanity.

With an excess of aerobic zeal we decided to walk back from the palace to the guest house. We found our way through the vast, cavernous, congested Pak Klong Talaat produce market, across a series of *klongs* (canals), and then for miles along the wide diagonal boulevard called Rama IV. It was about a six-mile walk. When we were only 300 yards from "home" we stopped and celebrated with dishes of ice cream.

January 10

At breakfast we met Peter and Peggy Ferry, middle-aged Plymouth Brethren missionaries on Phuket Island, 600 miles southwest of Bangkok. Phuket is adjacent to the Malay Peninsula and just below the Isthmus of Kra. He is Scottish; she is Malaysian. She is an intelligent, pleasant woman. When I asked how long they have been on the field, she said, "He 26 years; me 24." Did he go to the mission field single and meet her? Did his first wife die after only one or two years? As a young woman Peggy was a real beauty, I'm sure, and she is charming today.

Peter told me of a Pakistani Muslim whose father sent him to a training school. While he was there, preparing to evangelize Christians, he was required to read the New Testament. As he did so he became convinced that he was personally guilty before God and that he needed salvation. He accepted Christ; now he is a missionary to Muslims.

Peter also told me the story of a Buddhist, an alcoholic, a man who had once been a priest. One day as he was unsteadily riding his bicycle toward home, he became frightened by the heavy traffic and dismounted. He found himself in front of a Roman Catholic Church, and after pausing a moment, went in and sat down near the rear. It was cool. He rested his head on the back of a bench. When he opened his eyes, he saw a crucifix at the front of the church and began talking to it. "You're the only god I've never prayed to. Show me you're God by delivering me from alcohol." He wept, and continued talking to the figure on the cross. When he was finally sober, he rode home. The next day he had no desire for alcohol. Nor the next. After a week had gone by he still had no desire for it. "Jesus is God," he said. Later he joined a Plymouth Brethren group and is now a lay leader.

January 11

This was our last full day in Bangkok. Since a *klong* trip is a must, we boarded a long-tailed tour boat and headed upriver on the Chao Phya. It was a perfect day, sunny and pleasant. But then they're all perfect these days. We went past Wat Arun (Temple of the Dawn) with its high pagoda. After turning into a canal on the west side of the river, we ran for miles around bend after bend. Houses, mostly small and unpainted, stood on stilts along the water's edge. Palms, red and orange flowering trees, and greenery were everywhere. Exuberant tropical beauty. Interlacing canals of varying widths, small boats for family use, larger ones with goods. Sunlight and shadow. Waterside stores, with piers for customers' boats. Waterside temples. Small floating restaurants. A boat piled high with watermelons. People bathing (quite modestly), washing their hair, and washing dishes in the questionable canal water. Little children swimming some with suits, some without. Fishermen. Food preparation and games underway on patios. A dog asleep in a boat next to his master's porch. Here is a world in itself, a way of life.

We stopped alongside a canal in Thonburi and visited an ornate little temple. Even though it was small it possessed a remarkable sheen of beauty. Quite incongruously an audacious little black rooster strutted on a golden sill and seemingly considered himself lord of all he surveyed.

Then on a barge we were served many varieties of Thai fruit. Later a tug threw a line to the barge and began slowly pulling us on the second half of our journey. We saw a phalanx of red fireboats, apparently ready for instant duty; a girl alone in a small boat, looking up and waving at us; and a squadron of geese enjoying a watery front yard. Near the end of our trip as we went past the

Royal Barge National Museum, we saw eight splendid craft of a bygone era with their gilded bows pointed toward the canal.

I have never seen Venice, but now I don't need to go there. This was more colorful than Venice could ever be.

January 12

On this bright Sunday morning we walked a short distance to Christ Church. It is Anglican-Episcopal. With its high-arched nave and high open window arcades to allow air circulation, it is an intelligent adaptation of Gothic architecture to this tropical climate.

At the beginning of the service a girl of 12 or 13, clad in churchly robes, led the processional, bearing aloft a high wooden cross. She had an open, intelligent face and auburn hair in a thick braid that hung below her shoulders. Somehow she reminded me of Jean, our oldest grandchild. The sermon included a partial defense of infant baptism. While the defense was given with poise and flair, I was not convinced. To me, infant baptism is an unfortunate although perhaps inevitable corollary of the state-church system. And the state-church is not evident in the book of Acts. But then I am an Anabaptist and perhaps carry my own biases.

Impressions of Bangkok: no obesity; high-speed motorcycles, often with girls in skirts perched side-saddle on the buddy seats; three-wheeler open-air taxis (hold your hat!); exhaust fumes, tiny sidewalk eateries; a seemingly relaxed life-style; a blatant sex industry in the Patpong district; the klongs; the long-tailed boats; the glittering Grand Palace; the utterly jammed bazaars.

After a three and one-half hour flight to Bombay we found the Transit Hotel, a good place for us; we're going on to Pune tomorrow.

So we are back in vast, ancient, teeming India. Odors and scents, beauty and degradation, color and the gray face of poverty, mysticism and the grinding realities of humble vocations. We were here three weeks in '72 and for five months in '75-76. Now again.

India

Ten Weeks
In India

During our ten weeks we served at Union Biblical Seminary near Pune (Poona), 80 miles southeast of Bombay, and we traveled as tourists.

I had taught at UBS in '75-76 when it was located in Yavatmal, 400 miles east of Bombay. Since that time the seminary had been moved from isolated Yavatmal to its new Pune campus. Among the reasons for the move: a greater variety of churches in which students could do practical work, a better climate (Pune is higher than Yavatmal, though it can still get hot in late spring and summer), and broader cultural opportunities.

My courses at Pune were Matthew, Jeremiah, and Biblical Archaeology. The first was a new course for me but the others were old favorites. Doris worked indefatigably in the library, helping to accession thousands of books that for years had been overflowing a storage room. Using a typewriter held together by rubber bands, she typed about 7,000 cards.

In '72 and in '75-76 we had visited Delhi, Agra, Khajuraho, Varanasi, Patna, Ranchi, Raipur, Dhamtari, Jogdalpur, Sewagram, Indore, and Bombay. But we had never seen South India. This time therefore we took a five-day trip to Bangalore, Madurai, and Kodaikanal. And at the end of the ten weeks we spent 36 hours in Calcutta.

January 13

Just below our Bombay hotel window is a poverty scene. A dirt street — a playground and pig and dog habitat — between two rows of dilapidated buildings. Mud and stucco walls and corrugated metal roofs (some with old canvas on top). Open-air fires, naked children, and big sisters carrying little sisters and brothers. It gives a total impression of dirt, destitution, and privation. Yet I know there is much worse in Bombay.

Near the hotel this morning, and just outside the airport entrance, I walked past a tiny mudhole surrounded by rocks where six or eight women were flailing and pounding clothing. I have seen primitive washing scenes before but never anything like this. When I think of our immaculate washer and dryer standing side by side in our basement. . . .

Our Indian Airline plane for the short flight to Pune was an old 48-passenger turboprop. As we approached takeoff speed, the throttles were suddenly closed, and we came to a near-stop before taxiing by a roundabout route to our starting point. Then there was a great to-do in the cabin and beneath the engines by airline officials, engineers, the pilots, and would-be repairmen. Loud declamations and vigorous gestures indicated the intensity of the discussions. After 30 minutes however, without so much as the application of a screwdriver, we were back at the end of the runway, poised for another attempt. I wished Doris and I were somewhere else. But we got off the ground successfully and flew to Pune. The pilot may have shared my apprehensions, for the takeoff run was unusually long and the ascent quite tentative. No word of announcement was ever made — not even a "sorry for the delay." When I commented on this to the stewardess as we left the plane at Pune, she replied in astonishment, "But nothing happened!" The Mysterious East.

The seminary cab, a proud and venerable old conveyance, was waiting and took us to the new UBS location. It was great to see Saphir Athyal, the principal; his dark-haired wife, Sakhi; and their two vital teenagers, Vinie and Vidu. They are cherished friends from '75-76 and from their '79 visit to us in Indiana.

January 14

An interdenominational institution, Union Biblical Seminary has 215 students, most of them from India but some from other Southeast Asia countries. Everything here has been built since August 1979. The new location is a gently sloping plateau, halfway up a steep hillside just south of the major city of Pune.

As one looks up from the nearby village of Bibvewadi, the chapel with its prominent bell tower is especially prominent. Local people call it "the high church." They are referring to location, not liturgy. From the high ground of the campus great vistas lie to the south, west, and north. To the east on its higher hilltop is the imposing structure of the Medical Mission Sisters, a Roman Catholic convent group.

This evening Rosemary Wyse arrived. She is from Goshen, Indiana, and for three months will apply her professional library skills to the needy library here.

January 15

In chapel this morning a North India missionary told of his proposal to his wife. "I asked her, 'Would you be willing to share my poverty in missionary work?'" Whereupon the remarkable young lady replied, "I have had 15 proposals of marriage, and I have been waiting for one like this."

January 17

Just after nightfall, following the descending macadam road that connects the Medical Mission and the seminary with the main road in the village, I walked down to Bibvewadi to find a pharmacy. Suddenly I came upon two village women using the macadam as a latrine. They had no plumbing in their huts, of course, but other facilities and areas were available. Only ten feet away was a large and completely open field — and with no fence or ditch to complicate getting into it. But they were using the road where people must walk. It was an example of one side of India. A few minutes later I was in a pharmacy. It was small but neat, clean, and well-stocked. And I received courteous, efficient service. It was an example of another side of India.

January 19

The heavily accented English used by the students is a challenge. While some of the accent is British, some I suspect comes from one or another of the 15 languages of India. Then when one adds a British vocabulary, a different pitch, and rapid speech, the total effect can become bewildering. Sometimes I can get only two or three words of a sentence. I am guilty, I fear, of much hypocrisy nodding and saying "yes" when I don't really understand.

January 20

As I was jogging in a field, if that's the word for it, avoiding stones, holes, washouts, and low hummocks, three village women walked past. They looked at me in utter astonishment. I must have seemed like a visitor from another planet. But since they probably don't know about planets, maybe I seemed non-human or sub-human.

January 22

I often walk up the hill to the very crest — in the sunlight or early evening, or by moonlight or starlight. I like the wide panoramas, far horizons, and quietness.

On this delightful morning when I came back from a walk and found Doris in a pale yellow blouse and her Thai wraparound, I went for my camera. She stood between the climbing roses that festoon the outside steps to our apartment. Roses around her. A fitting frame.

January 25

At 6:45 a.m. as the eastern sky was red with sunrise and the western horizon was about to receive the pale full moon, we joined a group of students and faculty on the seminary lawn. The occasion was the annual observance of Republic Day. Saphir Athyal introduced Sister Matthew of the Medical Mission on the hill, the speaker of the occasion. After her brief address, both religious and patriotic in content, the flag of India was shaken free and saluted. Then a student read from Rabindranath Tagore, a Hindu poet, and another read Romans 13:1-7. At various intervals an officious student with the bearing and voice of a drill sergeant tried to bring us to attention. Some complied; others grinned and shuffled. The ceremony gave the impression of a nervous bonding of church and state, piety and patriotism.

January 28

This afternoon when I rode my rented bike south on the main highway that runs from Pune to far-distant Bangalore, I found myself barracked by trucks, buses, cars, motorbikes, motorcycles, and oxcarts. Drivers who were doing their best to cope with the heavy traffic regarded me with distaste if not hostility. Wind-driven dust clouds and black diesel contrails swirled around me. After four miles I said, "This is it," and turned back. It was no place for a bicycle.

January 29

In order that students may scatter out to local churches, regular Sunday services are not held on campus either in the morning or the evening. Instead, an all-campus worship service is scheduled each Wednesday afternoon from 5:00 to 6:30.

This afternoon an India bishop with a red sack vest and a stiff red and white collar spent nearly 50 minutes telling in a rambling sort of way his early missionary experiences in Africa. His talk had some merit — he told of humble beginnings of a mission program — but I would have preferred an expository message, and perhaps less vivid ecclesiastical habiliments.

At the table this evening Chuck Corwin, a visiting professor from California, quoted Saphir Athyal as saying, "No other person could possibly have done the initial building job for us at Pune that S. Paul Miller did." S. Paul is the missionary (now in retirement in Goshen, Indiana), who with prayer, skill, cajolery, and dogged determination put through the main building program here at the Pune campus. He had a genius for untangling, cutting, and by-passing red tape.

January 30

Our second floor apartment is one of the highest locations on campus. From our front porch we can look down across the lower campus and then for many miles to the southwest, over valleys, ravines, and partly-settled hill slopes — all the way to the impressive range of hills called The Western Ghats. From our bedroom and kitchen windows we can see at night below us to the north the great carpet of lights that is modern Pune. And each morning as we step out our front door we see the silhouette of the eastern hill against the sunrise. I said to Doris this morning, "Probably never again will we live in such a superb natural setting."

January 31

This evening Doris and I attended the student Music and Cultural program. One of the early numbers was the Mizo Bamboo Dance, performed with grace and verve by students from Nagaland in the Assam region of extreme northeastern India. We enjoyed this same dance three weeks ago at the Rose Gardens near Bangkok.

The feature of the evening was the drama, "Barabbas." Written by Dr. Chris Wright, a UBS prof now on sabbatical in England, it fleshes out the character of the insurrectionary who is presented with such brevity in the four gospels. Everything that could possibly go wrong in terms of curtains, lights, and sound did go wrong, but the student acting and Dr. Wright's script atoned for all the glitches. The students played their parts with poise, sensitivity, and intensity.

I think there must be ingredients in India culture that encourage vigorous theater. Perhaps one is the constant reenactment before entranced audiences in villages, towns, and cities of the epic Ramayana, that ancient tale of love, war, virtue, heroism, and triumph. Perhaps another is the frequent presentation of the classical dances that stem from India's vivid ancient mythology.

February 1

Partway downtown is an open area with the noble name of Salisbury Park. But the reality is ignoble. One sees uncut grass, a total absence of landscaping, trash blowing everywhere, stray goats and bullocks, pigs rooting in windrows of garbage, and people squatting, defecating.

My three-wheeler taxi driver this afternoon was a wild man, a Jehu. He just missed a little boy, just missed a taxi, and then hit a bicycle. Fortunately no one was injured and damage was minimal. My charioteer was completely in the wrong. Instead of going around a traffic island, he had cut inside it, and the bicyclist hadn't been able to get out of his way. The biker was understandably indignant, but my man was unfazed. As we started up again he had the gall to turn and say to me, "What can a person do?"

February 2

In mid-morning I walked to the hillcrest and then on through open country to the southeast. I descended into a valley, at times following small, barely-discernible winding paths through the short dry grass and at times picking my own route between boulders. Except for a few huts and bullocks at distant points and an occasional lonely tree, there was little to see. Here and there in a fold of the hills lay a small field where shallow ploughing had been done. On my return trip the sun was high, so was the temperature, and a host of flies were circling me. I thought of Noel Coward's "Only mad dogs and Englishmen go out in the noonday sun."

If on this February 2 Punxsutawney Phil, that almost legendary Pennsylvania groundhog, had been transported to Pune he most assuredly would have been alarmed by his shadow.

February 3

Today I met Edward and Ramoth Burkhalter, long-term General Conference Mennonite missionaries in India. I had known several of their gifted children at Goshen College, but I had never met the parents. After talking with them I said to myself, "Now I know where the Burkhalter children get their brains and personalities." Ed is a member of the UBS Board of Governors and he and Ramoth are here for a visit.

Ed and Ramoth recognize the benefits that have accrued to UBS from its move to Pune, but they also feel that the bigger campus and broader cosmopolitan culture may discourage students from accepting pastorates in small villages. If so, it would be unfortunate, but on the other hand city populations are expanding in India just as they are elsewhere in the world, and UBS graduates will be needed for India's growing cities.

The General Conference Mennonite mission area is east and northeast of Raipur, the Mennonite Brethren are located south of Hyderabad, and the Mennonite Church locations are south and east of Raipur and in western Bihar.

February 5

In India change-making is a major problem. Storekeepers want you to hand over the exact amount in notes (bills) and coins. They may not actually have any paise, the pennies of India, or small rupee notes with which to give change. Or if they do they're reluctant to part with them. When one gives a clerk a ten rupee note for something that costs 9.60 rupees, it's common for the clerk to hesitate, then ask if you have the exact amount, and if you don't, for him to scurry next door with your note or down the street to a bank or hotel or larger store to get help. Or he might offer you stamps or coughdrops to make things come out even.

I asked a man on the street, "Why this shortage of small change?"

"There are many beggars in India," he replied. "They get the change; they keep it."

When I mentioned this to an Indian professor at the seminary, he said, "That is perhaps partly true, but the biggest factor is that the government simply doesn't put enough money into the expensive process of printing small notes and minting coins."

February 7

Tonight in Matthew class we went over 5:43-48. After finishing the exposition, I spoke somewhat as follows: "It is partly on the basis of Matthew 5:43-48 that I am a pacifist. Other key references are Luke 6:27-28, John 18:36, Romans 12:14-21, and I Peter 2:19-21. I cannot get away from these passages. They make me try to be a pacifist. Sometimes I fail. While I don't swing my fists, I have used words as fists and have had to repent.

"Pacifism has problems — for example, when one's country is invaded by an evil national power, or when one's wife or family is attacked by an evil person. I have not adopted pacifism because it is an easy position either to apply or defend. I have adopted it because of the above sections in the New Testament, and because it seems incredible that members of Christ's spiritual Kingdom in one nation should kill members of that Kingdom in another nation. Applying pacifism gives me problems, but I couldn't face myself if I would ignore New Testament language.''

With courtesy, and even intentness, the students heard me out. Perhaps that's all a pacifist can ask.

February 8

While processing errands in downtown Pune, Rosemary and I had to detour into the Old City for gamma globulin. We flagged down a three-wheeler and soon found ourselves in the clangorous complexity of Lakshmi Road. Almost every conceivable type of vehicle vied for space and progress in the street. And vegetables, fruits, and garlands of all colors were on display on the sidewalks. Turgid streams of people, most of them women in bright saris, filled in the rest of the scene. I thought I had already seen the ultimate in compressed color and commercial congestion. I hadn't seen this.

February 14

Yesterday Rosemary, Doris, and I flew to Bangalore on the first leg of our trip to visit the John Nyces of Goshen, Indiana, at Kodaikanal in South India. We stayed last night in the Shilton Hotel. It was not quite a Hilton.

After visiting the Lalbaugh Gardens this morning (they were too bare, too dry), we went to Mahatma Ghandi and Brigade Roads for shopping. I more or less tagged along, but I did find a book with the text of Satyajit Ray's film trilogy — ''Pather Panchali,'' ''Aparajito,'' and ''The World of Apu.'' Years ago I saw the first and the third of these and loved them.

In this trilogy Ray, a Bengali director, conveyed a special angle of vision toward life in Bengal (East Bengal is now Bangladesh and West Bengal is in eastern India). Above everything else, Ray sought realism — in physical settings, attire, gestures, turns of speech, emotions, and incidents. The result in his trilogy is a mosaic of Bengali village life. The three films gave Ray worldwide status as a director.

In the afternoon we flew to Madurai, and I was soon bargaining with a taxi driver for the 90-mile run to Kodai. We settled on 510 rupees (about $40 U.S.) and off we went.

For part of the way we drove through a lush rural area. Tall palms lined the road. And to our left and right, beyond green rice paddies and high stands of sugar cane, we saw groves of coconut palms. We went through little villages with thatched roofs, lazy bullocks, playing children, blooming bougainvillaea, and carefully swept bare yards. Further along we drove past threshing floors where winnowing was in process and great piles of rice straw lay heaped on the ground.

We saw men striding determinedly with large quantities of straw on their shoulders, women gently swaying along with piles of wood or fodder — or with big brass water-pots — on their heads, and bicyclists struggling to stay upright in spite of precariously balanced bales of cane on their small rear carriers. It was pastoral and picturesque, but oh the physical labor involved in such panoramas.

Just before dark we left the plains and started up into the mountains. At the base of the first ridge we were at about 1,000 feet, but in the next two hours we went up another 6,500, around many hundreds of curves. About ten minutes below Kodaikanal we stopped briefly at the Silver Cascade, an impressive 80-foot waterfall. It was lovely in the darkness. As we were standing at its base two cars rounded the nearby curve and briefly illuminated it with their headlights.

We received a warm welcome from the Nyces. During their Goshen College sabbatical John and Dorothy Nyce are serving here as teachers and houseparents at the International School. Lynda and Gretchen, their teenage daughters, are attending the school and seem to be flourishing in the Kodai environment.

February 15

Kodaikanal is in the Indian state of Tamil Nadu. I was told today that about 16% of Tamil Nadu's population is classified as Christian. In the nearby state of Kerala the figure is over 30%, and in one or two of the small states or union territories in the Assam region the percentage is amazingly high — about 90%. But in India as a whole less than 4% of the population is regarded as Christian in religious affiliation. What is the population of India? Over 800,000,000.

In this vast land there are 15 official languages. Hindi, for example, is the language of four states: Madhya Pradesh, Uttar Pradesh, Bihar, and Haryana. Marati is spoken in the state of Maharashtra, Bengali is spoken in West Bengal, Tamil in Tamil Nadu, and Telegu in Andhra Pradesh.

Next door to the Nyces is a cottage called "Wissahickon," the Indian name of a little stream in eastern Pennsylvania. Perhaps the cottage name was chosen many decades ago by a homesick teacher.

In 1952 while Royal and Evelyn Bauer, missionaries in India, were staying at Wissahickon, she contracted an illness that at first was thought to be malaria but that was soon diagnosed as polio. When the dread word was spoken, there was no time to lose. Vellore, the nearest major hospital (Dr. Ida Scudder's), was 300 miles away — 300 miles of poor roads. A station wagon was found, a small support group chosen for the trip, and a mattress placed in the back for Evelyn. In late afternoon, June 1, the desperate journey began. They drove through the night and into the morning.

At Vellore her condition worsened and she was put in an iron lung. One of those with Royal and Evelyn on that night trip was Blanche Sell, my wife's sister, a missionary nurse in India 1949-84. In late July Evelyn was able to fly to Bombay and on to the U.S. where she partially regained muscle strength. Evelyn has told her story with sensitivity in *Through Sunlight and Shadow*, Herald Press, 1959.

February 16

Due to recent heavy rains here at Kodai everything is green. These February rains have surprised me. I thought a dry season extended over all of India until the great northward-sweeping monsoons of May and June. John Nyce tells me however that southern India has its own rainfall pattern.

In spite of suffering from the affliction known to English and American residents as "Delhi belly," I went along this afternoon on a tour of the Kodai highlands. We saw forests, terraced hillsides, pear and plum trees in bloom, giant eucalyptus trees, and mists and clouds sweeping up across the hillsides and treetops. At several places we could look far down and away to the distant plains, and at one point we saw a slender cascade falling many hundreds of feet into the green forest below.

February 17

Long before daybreak we were on our way by taxi to meet our plane. We drove down from the mountains by a "back road," with the macadam strip descending steeply in an extraordinary series of switchbacks, and then across the plains to Palni — we saw its temple high atop an enormous boulder — and on to the Coimbatore airport. We arrived back at the seminary in early evening.

February 19

Imshen Tushimeren came to the house this evening for a makeup quiz in the Matthew class. In his home church in the hills of Nagaland near the northeastern tip of India he has served as a youth leader. Now for two years he has been at UBS. He is 36, unmarried, hardworking, and devoted to Christ's Kingdom. Partly because of the English language medium, seminary studies are difficult for him. But he is undaunted. His big problem is whether to come back for a third year. His inclination is to return, but his church superintendent at home is urging him to cut short his studies and take up his youth work again.

"We have found no one to replace you."

In a few weeks Imshen will go back to Nagaland for at least the summer. He will travel 38 hours by rail via Bombay to Calcutta, 38 more into Assam, and then two days by bus into the hill country. There he will have to make his decision.

February 21
From the hilltop at sunset one can see the sun go down behind the distant, sharp-angled, blue line of the Western Ghats. Then the light fades rapidly, but about 30 minutes later a great afterglow of red and orange blooms in the western sky.

February 22
Today Mr. Borde, a seminary teacher, took several of us on a tour of Pune. "What is the population of Pune?" I asked him.

"Eleven lakhs," he replied. That is, 1,100,000. *Lakh* is the Hindi word for 100,000 and it has been transposed into the British English that is used across much of India.

Among the places to which he took us was the old Central Prison, an enormous layout behind almost endless gray walls. We visited the three adjacent cells where in 1930-32 Mahatma Ghandi, Jawarhalal Nehru, and Nehru's father, Motilal Nehru, were imprisoned by the British. I am sure the rooms look better today than they did then. To the people of the independent nation of India they are now historical shrines. In fact, a bust of the Mahatma stands on a pedestal in a small garden just outside his cell.

We also went to the commune of Shree Rajneesh Bhagwan. Only about 60 of the Bhagwan's followers remain, but during his heyday here in the 70s (before he relocated at Antelope, later called Rajneeshpuram, Oregon) there were thousands. They came from all over the world and lived at the commune, at the nearby Blue Diamond Hotel, and at any place near at hand where lodging could be found. The Bhagwan's daily lectures, a mix of eastern mysticism, western philosophy, pop psychology, and sexual libertinism, were taped and printed and now fill hundreds of volumes. With their bright covers and eye-catching titles, all the volumes, filling shelf after shelf, are displayed for sale in the bookstore inside the commune entrance.

Near the main gate is a sign. "A community to provoke God." While I assume India English might define "to provoke" as "to stimulate" or " to excite" or "to gain a response from," I suspect God is provoked in the blunt American sense of the word.

February 23

Today Saphir Athyal told me how his Vidu, then age 5, once offered to teach Hindi to Jake Enz, a visiting American prof and a Johns Hopkins Ph.D. Vidu said he would give Jake one new word each day, with the stipulation that at the time of the daily "lesson" Jake would have to repeat all the words from previous days. On the fourth day Jake stumbled over an earlier word and Vidu said sadly, "Uncle, you are a hopeless student!"

February 24

Between classes and at night I am reading Lapierre's *The City of Joy*. The title is the English translation of Anand Nagar, the Bengali name of a jammed and filthy slum within Calcutta. Here 70,000 people live "on an expanse of ground hardly three times the size of a football field" (p. 45). When we visit Calcutta a month from now, we will try to go into Anand Nagar.

February 26

Chuck Corwin — who has served as a missionary in Japan — and I were talking today about the American occupation of Japan in the late 1940s. After we discussed briefly how favorably MacArthur's reforms and administration were accepted by the Japanese people,

Chuck told of a Honshu farmer who with a patriotism splendidly uninformed by history said, "The Emperor couldn't have found a better man."

March 1

Saphir Athyal, the principal of UBS, is a visionary, a driver, a workaholic, a man who gets things done. He saw the need to move the seminary from Yavatmal to Pune and got it accomplished. I doubt if anyone else could have pulled it off. He has an Old Testament doctorate from Princeton, a personal charisma, a great capacity for teaching and story-telling, and the respect of the students. And he is not an international transplant; he is Indian.

However, as John L. Stauffer used to say to me, "Every prince in Israel limps." Saphir finds it almost impossible to delegate authority; he will only give departmental independence to a tough-minded individual who is willing to stand up to him. He will then praise such persons for what they accomplish, even if he has criticized their procedures in the meantime. With subordinates in general Saphir has a strong tendency to disagree or make counter-suggestions. If someone buys something for the seminary, he will almost invariably say, "You paid too much for it." In a jesting way Chuck once suggested to him that he have a card printed up with those words and then simply hand it out after a purchase was made. Saphir laughed good-naturedly.

These difficulties in relating to others have produced an escalating tension between him and his faculty. Others of course have not been blameless. In response to the state of tension the governing board has apparently indicated to Saphir that next year should be his last. He has done much for UBS; it will be extremely difficult to replace him.

March 3

At 5:30 a.m. a stupid dog was sitting in the moonlight on the athletic field, 60 yards from my window, endlessly barking at nothing. Finally I pulled on a pair of pants and went out and threw rocks at him. Unfortunately I missed every time. This campus is cursed with nondescript curs.

I got dressed then and walked up the hill in the early dawn light. I stood on the hilltop facing the sunrise and had my daily prayer time.

March 5

For some time I have been baffled by a sign in Salisbury Park. On a gray wall in white paint is the neatly done likeness of a bicycle, and next to it is the exhortation, "Stamp on Cycle." More than once I tried in vain to imagine what manner of communication was intended here. Since a vast abundance of bicycles swerve in and out of traffic lanes, it even occurred to me that this might be a call to jihad against two-wheelers.

Now the mystery has been solved. A friend told me that a bicycle is the symbol of a political party, just like the Democrat donkey and the G.O.P. elephant. "Stamp on Cycle" is a plea to vote for that party. To "stamp" is to affix one's vote on election day.

Herewith a phrasing in an Indian newspaper: The scandal at Bombay University "became further hotter." And the following wording appeared in a newspaper matrimonial advertisement: "A beautiful, homely girl." Mr. Daniel, the seminary Business Manager, tells me that in India a "homely" girl or woman is an expert in domestic science.

On this visit in India I haven't yet seen my favorite highway signs from '72 and '75-76: "Speed Slowly" and "Dead Slow."

March 8

This evening John, Dorothy, Lynda, and Gretchen Nyce arrived from Kodaikanal for a three-day stay. Dorothy, who chairs the Overseas Committee of our Mission Board, is interested in visiting this interdenominational campus that is partially supported by the Board, and John is working on an India missions and seminary photography project.

March 9

At 8:00 on this Sunday morning Doris, Dorothy, John, and I went to Oldham Methodist Church. Also with us was Ruth Rani Boutique, the petite Mennonite Brethren seminary girl from Hyderabad. Oldham is her local church and she is one of the students John is featuring in his UBS photography. Ruth sang a solo while John wielded his camera and flash unit.

In the Oldham services — this is our second or third visit — I have felt a partial lack of vitality. Everything is in English, to begin with. While that is fine for people like us, the atmosphere, not only in language but also in singing and worship, seems more Western than Eastern, more English than Indian.

Then we walked to St. Andrews Hindustani Covenant Church for a slightly later morning service. There we met Prabakhar Singh, a seminary student from Dhamtari who is also being featured by John. He and other UBSers sang as a group in the worship period. The service was in Hindustani — a North India language, a mix of Hindi and Urdu — and the music had Indian elements. All around me I sensed elements of vibrancy and color. A more thorough transplantation of Christianity into Indian culture was present than at Oldham, and as a result a greater vitality. Or so it seemed to me.

March 10

I'm not eagerly awaiting the next 14 days, the last part of our UBS assignment. The afternoons are hot, and getting hotter; I will have 105 exam papers to grade, each with eight essay questions; and I won't enjoy encounters with classroom lawyers who want to make a federal case out of their grades. I remember several such confrontations at Yavatmal in '76.

At 4:00 Doris, Dorothy, Gretchen, John, and I went

for tea at Prabakhar and Vasti's apartment. We are impressed with this young couple. She is sweet, dedicated, sensible. He is earnest and balanced. He wants to serve as a pastor and not become enmeshed in the tangled church situation at Dhamtari. That of course will be difficult.

March 12

Rosemary Wyse was caught this afternoon in the middle of a huge dust-devil that came whirling across campus. In his office in the Ad Building Saphir heard her scream, flung up his window, and there she was, right in the vortex of a minor cyclone, with dust and paper swirling furiously around her. In emulation of Elisha, as Elijah ascended to heaven in a whirlwind with chariots and horses of fire, Saphir began chanting, "My father, my father, the chariots of Israel and its horsemen!" Unhurt but disheveled, Rosemary detoured home for a shower, shampoo, and a new outfit.

It's hard to take the afternoon heat. The temperature at 4:00 p.m. must have been close to 100 degrees. With the high ceilings and the fans it's endurable but that's about all.

March 15

Roger Wood, a Friends teacher from Ohio, and I met at the Administration Building an hour before sunrise and started up the hill. We wanted to see if Halley's Comet was visible. Until our eyes were accustomed to the darkness and we had left behind the Bibvewadi village lights, we made no attempt to spot it. But as we approached the hill crest and began scanning the southeastern sky, there it was! It was not brilliant but it was clearly discernible. It had a star-like point of light at its head and a luminous tail. Ever since I was a boy and heard Dad talk about Halley's Comet, I wanted to see it. 1986 seemed far distant. But now both the year and the comet have come.

In 1910 when it made a close approach to the earth and when Dad was 19, he saw it one morning at the peak of its splendor. Not long before sunrise he looked from his bedroom window and saw the glowing head just above the horizon and the translucent tail, pale lemon in color, flaring toward the zenith.

This afternoon Doris and I visited Ravi Shankar Rao and his wife Mary, and their daughter Tabitha. He was raised in a Hindu home but became a Christian seven years ago when he was 25. Since his conversion his mother has come to Christ and now his youngest sister is close to a decision. He arrived at UBS a year ago and has been working hard on his English proficiency. Mary is also picking up English.

Little Tabitha, four, was entranced by Doris' photograph album. She played with it and was determined to keep it. She held it close to her breast with both arms and beseeched with a smile and with her big dark eyes. When her parents made her yield it up at the end of our visit, she cried. We will give them a picture of us. Rao has a quiet charisma and strength, and his wife is poised and gracious. He has a call to minister to the people of his background.

March 16

At 3:30 Doris and I took a cab to the base of the Parvati Hindu temple. It was a hot, steep ascent. Apart from good views of Bibvewadi and Pune, there wasn't much to see when we did get to the top. The grounds are unkempt and dirty and the temple architecture is undistinguished. On its high hill two miles northwest of the seminary it looks much more impressive than it does close at hand.

March 20

Just before sunrise yesterday 18 of us went up the hill to see Halley's Comet. Doris and I, the Athyals, several teachers, and a few campus visitors made up the group. I thought the comet was a bit brighter than when Roger and I saw it a few days ago.

I'm working almost nonstop on grading final exam

essay questions. UBS has a core of superb students, people who would flourish in doctoral programs in any major English or American university. Others have less ability and are also partially handicapped in English. And some fracture English and rearrange knowledge most marvelously.

March 21

I worked until 1:20 a.m. on exams and have now finished 70 of the 105. At midnight I took a break and walked up the hill. The moon, just past the half and directly overhead, splendidly illuminated the hilltop.

March 22

With his new and powerful steed my three-wheeler cabbie this evening broke all existing limits and considered it absolutely craven to miss anyone or anything by more than two inches. I must admit however that he had good reflexes; he never even scraped paint.

Just yesterday a cobra was killed at a point only 100 feet from our steps. It was found in the rocks above the new athletic field and close beside the little campus roadway where we walk.

March 24

Last night at 7:40 I finished my last essay question and at 10:30 handed in all my papers and grades to the Director of Studies. Without Doris' help I couldn't have met the deadline; she graded the objective questions and did all the averaging. She is a great co-worker. At 6:00 this morning we left for the airport and Calcutta via Bombay.

I'll miss the student and faculty fellowships, the deep joy of teaching Bible here, the splendid campus location, the mellow evenings, my rambles on the hill, and the color and vitality of Pune. And yes, I'll miss the lugubrious, plaintive, eloquent dissonances of the donkeys on the flats just below us to the north.

I didn't see much terrain on the Bombay-Calcutta

flight (it was hazy) until we began our descent over West Bengal. Then I saw green fields and paddies, flat countryside, canals and irrigation ditches, and lazily curving rivers. Soon we crossed the Hoogli River and banked right for our landing.

The evening air was hot when we stepped out of the airport terminal. My first impressions of Calcutta on the taxi ride at dusk to the Mennonite Central Committee house were of innumerable open-air cooking fires, miserable hutments, and a smoky, murky, fetid atmosphere.

Peter and Margaret Peters, the MCC directors here, gave us a splendid welcome. After the evening meal Peter and I took a short walk. We went west to Park Circus, where Hasari Pal of *The City of Joy* often waited for rickshaw customers, and then turned northwest on Park Street to Lower Circular Road. On the crowded sidewalks men, women, and children lay sleeping on strips of cloth or burlap, oblivious to traffic, horns, lights, and masses of pedestrians. "That's home," Peter said. We watched rickshaw pullers perspiring in the hot night, pulling their human burdens up and down the street at a half-run. "I don't think I could ever let myself be pulled in one of those," I said. "And yet I suppose the men desperately need the money."

"That's right," Peter answered.

When we were ready to go back, we talked it over briefly and then squeezed onto a rickshaw seat for the half-mile return trip. I watched our "human horse," a term often used for these men, and thought again of Hasari Pal.

At the end of the journey the puller asked for 20 rupees. Peter smiled and said gently, "You have worked hard." Indeed he had. The sweat was pouring from him. "But usually you would get three or four rupees for this trip; isn't that right?" Peter was speaking kindly, and the rickshaw man assented with a grin and a nod. "But I'm going to give you ten." I added the few small coins I had in my pocket. Later Peter said, "That's only the second time I've ridden in one, but I thought you should discover tonight what it's like."

March 25

At 8:15 we attended the morning devotional period at the Mennonite Central Committee office. We sang "My Hope Is Built On Nothing Less" and recited together a written prayer. A few of the lines we recited were these:

"So we bring our prayers to You:

For those who suffer pain...

For those who are satisfied with something less than the life for which they were made...

For those who know that they must shortly die;

For those who cannot wait to die...."

They seemed so fitting for the realities of Calcutta.

In India the MCC is headquartered in Calcutta, and much of its humanitarian work — such as educational assistance and special vocational training — is done here, but agricultural programs are carried out at various places in India. I believe Peter H. Peters and his staff work creatively to meet human need and also work in careful cooperation with the Indian authorities.

In mid-morning as we left the Thai Airways office and walked toward our MCC car, a pathetic young man with one leg completely off and the other amputated at the knee reached up and asked for money. Since I don't usually give to beggars I turned away, but then with amazing agility and determination he scuttled crablike across the street, reached up, and managed to open the car door. I relented and gave him a small rupee note. Then after we were in the car and the door was shut, he gave guidance with arm waves to our driver as he backed our car into the busy intersection. As I thought of the young man's almost incredible resolve to make his way, I was both moved and ashamed. I'm afraid I had acted the part of the haughty tourist or The Ugly American.

We spent a short time in Anand Nagar, the terrible slum in Lapierre's book. We saw enormous mudholes, muddy lanes with huts on both sides, bullocks, heaps of manure, tiny shops, and crowded sidewalks. When I was reading *The City of Joy* in Pune, I said to myself, "I wonder if the descriptions aren't exaggerated, if the author hasn't engaged in literary overkill. But here in Calcutta I was told, "No, Lapierre hasn't overdrawn the picture; his book is realistic." Now I have seen part of Anand Nagar myself.

For years we have read about Mother Teresa, the radiant Albanian nun who years ago left the comfortable Loreto Convent in Calcutta to heed "a call within a call," the summons to serve "the poorest of the poor." Today was our chance to see her Home for the Destitute and the Dying, a shelter where the poor and the desperately ill can receive Christian love. Our visit was brief; we did not wish to intrude on busy service patterns. A young woman from Boston, a seven-week volunteer, took us through the men's and women's wards. The Home for the Destitute and the Dying is a fulfillment of Jesus' words in Matthew 25:34-40. In fact, it is an incarnation. Jesus is the Word made flesh; the Home is the words of Matthew 25:34-40 made flesh.

Then we walked 100 yards to the Temple of Kali, the fiercest of the gods in the Hindu pantheon. She "demands sacrifices and wears a garland of skulls," say Crowther, Raj, and Wheeler in their guidebook on India. We saw dirt, disorder, sleeping dogs, and uncouth devotees. The Home and the Temple are physically close; otherwise, they are far apart.

In Calcutta live 12 ½ million people. "It is a city of refugees," someone told me. The human needs are so vast that they could absorb for generations the efforts of a host of servants.

Tomorrow is Holi, the exuberant annual festival that marks the coming of spring. It is celebrated by throwing colored liquids and powders at anyone and everyone. Since we are to leave tomorrow, Doris and I decided to go to the Airport Hotel tonight and to avoid tomorrow's gauntlet of gaudy liquids. The colors of Holi, we've been told, are hard to wash out.

March 26

When I tried to buy a postcard last night at the hotel souvenir shop, all I could find were Russian postcards. Yes, Russian. They were monotones of uninspiring buildings in Russia. I bought one and mailed it to Dad and Mom in Pennsylvania. "No, we're not in Russia," was my opening line.

Once again we say good-bye to India. This land fascinates me. Some things are repellent, but land and people call to me. Here are mighty rivers, great mountains, and noble human monuments — the matchless Taj Mahal, for example, and the superb wall paintings of the Ajanta caves. I like rice and curry (though not three times a day), the femininity of saris, and the courtesy of chance acquaintances. Above all, I sense the vibrant will of multitudes to cope and survive, and I respond to the elemental beauty of unchanging agricultural panoramas.

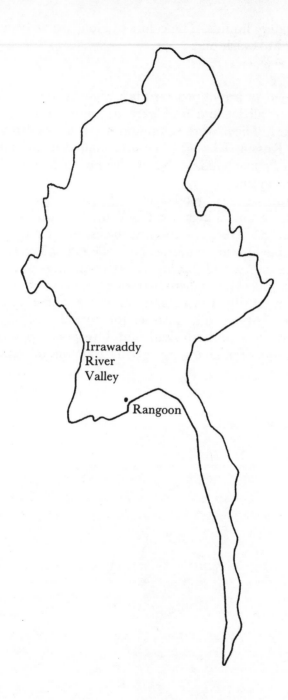

Irrawaddy
River
Valley

Rangoon

Burma

Six Days
In Rangoon

J ust before we left Japan in December 1985, the Mennonite Board of Missions in Indiana asked us to spend a
week in Rangoon, Burma. After some rearranging of our
teaching and flight schedules, we were able to fit in this
visit. The request came from the Board because of a small
struggling church in Rangoon (I'll call it the Bethel
Fellowship) which wants to affiliate with the Mennonite
Church. In 1984 Norman Kraus spent several days with
the Fellowship, and now the Board wished us to further
investigate the group, befriend it, and in general keep
lines of communication open.

From Calcutta we flew to Bangkok, stayed one night at
the Christian Guest House, stored surplus baggage at the
airport, and then took off for Rangoon. We looked forward to this Rangoon visit, partly because of interest in
the Bethel Fellowship and partly because of curiosity
about the backward land of Burma. I had picked up (in
India) the January 20, 1986 ''Time'' and had found an
article on Burma. ''For more than a generation,'' it said
in the opening paragraph, ''the country has existed in a
time warp — and in a state of solitary confinement . . .
foreigners have been unwelcome, borders have been
tight, private business has been discouraged, and
development has all but halted.'' A little further along it
asserted, ''If Burma did not exist, Evelyn Waugh would
have had to invent it.''

March 27

Zaw David of the Fellowship met us at the airport and took us to the Strand Hotel. In the "Time" article we had seen a photograph of this old hotel and the accompanying caption. "Among the sepia-toned relics, the Strand Hotel stands as a grand monument to colonial decay." Decay? Perhaps, but our room is big, clean, and pleasant, and it even has an air-conditioner. We are thankful for it. Rangoon steams with heat and humidity.

After dinner I went for a walk in the hot twilight. The hotel is close to the Rangoon River but is almost completely blocked off from it by weary-looking warehouses and docks. Riverside parks and esplanades seem nonexistent.

March 28

This morning Lisana Edward, as I will call him, a member of the Fellowship, came for us and we left by taxi. Our conveyance, a small pickup with wooden benches in the back and a rudimentary roof overhead, took us past crumbling sidewalks and unpainted buildings to the gold-covered Schwedagon Pagoda, the highest pagoda in the world, and the chief Buddhist shrine of Burma. We saw Buddhas in abundance, seated and reclining, and at least an acre of gold leaf.

Our next stop was the zoo — not as capricious a choice as might be thought. Apparently churches and their leaders are subject to surveillance, especially when a foreigner makes contact with them. Moreover, there was reason to suspect that our hotel room might be bugged, and so Lisana was seeking a spot where we could talk in private. He found it. We sat on a bench near the baboon cages. While the baboons shrieked and howled in the near background, we talked about the churches in Burma — their problems, successes, and needs. Doris and I asked in particular about the theological views of the Fellowship, the backgrounds of its members, its relationships with other churches, and its worship patterns, evangelistic work, and finances. He had many questions of course for us. He asked us about the history, polity, doctrine, and practice of our church. We tried to answer.

At one point during our two hours there a gentleman came, sat down near us, and began reading a newspaper. I wondered about him, but our brother did not seem concerned, and therefore I wasn't either — not much, at least. In any case there was nothing seditious about our conversation. Lisana is obviously a loyal citizen of Burma and I certainly have no designs upon the integrity of the government.

One of the Burmese young women at the hotel desk has long jet-black hair. Caught in a single heavy braid, it falls to her knees, alongside her long wraparound skirt ("longhi"). She posed for Doris and me beside the desk today. I think I got a good picture. In the late evening under a moon that was just one day past full, Doris and I walked east to the Botataung Pagoda. It was closed of course but the moonlight was gleaming on its high golden spire.

March 29

This morning at a nearby church we met with the Bethel Fellowship. Since foreign ministers are not supposed to preach in Burma, I simply gave a "testimony" in regard to my conversion, and then I gave a second testimony on Acts 10:34-43. Doris spoke too. We worked through an interpreter.

The Bethel Fellowship has a core group of 15 to 20 persons. For the most part these are people who still have their memberships in established congregations but who are now pouring their energies into child Christian education and adult evangelism. Their theology is conservative and their emphases very practical. They speak much of the new birth and assurance. Since they tend to be critical of the older Protestant churches ("They don't emphasize the new birth and evangelism"), they feel it necessary to go it alone and ultimately to become a new church. They feel a need for "a mother church" and for financial assistance from outside.

It is hot, hot, hot. "The Guardian," Rangoon's daily English newspaper, reported that yesterday it was 103 degrees and that this was 6 or 7 degrees "below normal." Let's hear it for subnormalcy.

March 30

After a bout of nausea and vomiting last night, I was low on energy today (Sunday) and spent much of the day resting. In the evening Doris went with Zaw David to a large Baptist church. Over 500 were present, she reported, and there was great singing. She was introduced and at the request of the program leader spoke words of Christian greeting.

Doris is such a good wife and traveling companion and co-worker. I "lucked out" when I found her 47 years ago. No, God led us together.

March 31

This morning we took a taxi to the east side of Rangoon and met with a Baptist leader. His data on the religious patterns of Burma were quite helpful and supplemented other information we have received.

Burma has about 35,000,000 people. Of these about 87% are Buddhist and about 5% are Christian. Baptists constitute the largest Christian block. Roman Catholics are second, followed by Methodists and Anglicans. Most Burmese live in the Irrawaddy River valley (the central valley of the land) and in the Irrawaddy delta. This is the agricultural heartland of the nation and here Buddhism is strongest. By contrast, Christianity has rooted itself most deeply among the tribes in the hill regions that ring the valley in a great arc from southeast to north to southwest. Large numbers of Karens, Shans, Kachins, Nagas, and Chins have accepted the Christian faith. In fact, the majority of Karens and Kachins are Christian. The former religion of the hill tribes was animism (the worship and placating of the spirits who dwell in trees, rocks, waterfalls, mountains, and other phenomena of nature). Among these hill people the Good News has found a far greater acceptance than among the Buddhists of the central valley.

April 1

Today Doris and I visited a Bible Society bookstore. "It's the only Christian bookstore in Burma," someone told me. The shelves however were nearly empty. No Burmese Bibles at all were on hand. Only in the languages of several of the hill tribes were Bibles available.

How shall I analyze the Bethel Fellowship and what recommendation, if any, shall I make to the Elkhart Board? The Fellowship people are earnest Christians and have a warm piety. They are witnesses for Christ. It is obvious that they have needs. Their frank requests for help do not at all turn me off; in their situation I would ask as they do. While it is probable that they overemphasize some elements of Christian experience at the expense of others, they are broad-spirited and willing to learn. I think they may be over-critical of the older churches. But this is a complicated issue; sometimes God raises up new movements to revitalize older ones.

Should the Mennonite Church invite the Bethel Fellowship into Mennonite World Conference, and should our Elkhart Mission Board include the Fellowship's needs in a broad way in its annual budgets? People with a broader background than I in church extension will have to answer those questions, but my heart and my spirit say, "In some way, somehow, we must help the Fellowship."

April 2

Eating our meals at the Strand has given us contact with other visitors to Burma — with people who have varied insights.

This morning I saw a number of paintings by local artists. Many of them were of elemental, vital up-country scenes and panoramas. I wish we could stay longer in Burma. Going up the Irrawaddy and getting into the hill country would be a wholesome counter-balance to the urban blight we have seen in Rangoon.

Our airport departure was not without tension. Through a perusal of tourist data I had become aware that the Burmese authorities have arrogated to themselves the privilege of confiscating manuscripts at the airport. And in my book bag I had several hundred pages of journal from Hong Kong, Bangkok, and India, to say nothing of the pages I had written in Rangoon. But all went with reasonable smoothness and we boarded our plane without literary molestation.

For both citizens and tourists Burma has no lack of regulations. Only about 100 tourists a day are admitted and visas are issued for only seven days. Major restrictions have been placed upon incoming goods such as used clothing, blankets, books, and even medical supplies. Limited amounts of material however can be carried in by tourists. At the Christian Guest House in Bangkok we were asked to take with us a number of religious books and also a packet of medicines, and we did so. The latter were needed by the wife of a church administrator, and it gave us a good feeling to deliver them at the Rangoon church office. Incidentally, many medicines can only be obtained in Burma through the black market or via special tourist delivery.

In the 1960s all Protestant and Roman Catholic missionaries were requested to leave, and mission schools and hospitals were nationalized. While it is forbidden to mail Burmese Bibles into the country, some individuals abroad do so — one Bible at a time.

Few Burmese can gain permission to leave the country. Mail is intercepted. Surveillance is tight. According to the January 20, 1986 "Time" article, a Western diplomat in Rangoon said, "There aren't many things the government does well, but putting down dissent is one of them."

With these somber words the "Time" article closes: "For the moment, it seems, Burma will continue to remain a never-never land where history is held under house arrest, and all the clocks have stopped."

Singapore in its Geographical Context

Five Weeks
In Singapore

At the 1984 Mennonite World Conference in Strasbourg, France, Doris and I met Charles Christano of Kudus, Indonesia. He was serving as moderator of the Strasbourg conference and was concluding his six-year term as MWC President. During the two weeks that followed, Charles and Lisa traveled with our tour group in Egypt, Jordan, and Israel. One day Charles said, "You must come to Indonesia; we want you to speak in our churches."

When our 1985-86 schedule was being arranged, Earl Martin of the Mennonite Central Committee, Akron, Pennsylvania, asked Charles to arrange for a block of our time during the spring of '86. Charles did this with vigor and efficiency and as a result we served for five weeks at the Discipleship Training Centre in Singapore (where Charles had once studied) before going on to Indonesia for an additional five weeks.

At the Center I taught two of my favorite courses, Jeremiah and Psalms, and Doris helped in the library. We also toured portions of Singapore and briefly visited the southern tip of Malaysia.

April 3

Yesterday we flew from Rangoon to Bangkok, picked up the luggage we had left at the airport a week earlier, and boarded a Thai Airways night flight to Singapore.

On the plane I got into a conversation with a young Muslim who was somewhat of a theological liberal. "Absolute religious knowledge is not possible," he informed me. Then he said, "I'm into meditation. It's wonderful to be set free of all biases." We had quite a to and fro for the next hour. Before leaving the plane we promised each other to do reading in the Koran and the New Testament.

Howard Peskett, dean of the Discipleship Training Centre, had written that he would meet us at the airport, but when we could not find anyone who looked like a theological dean, we took a taxi to the Centre.

From what we saw on our 30-minute trip, Singapore seems to be a modern metropolis. We also saw lush greenery and the fringes of parks at a number of points. The contrast with Rangoon is almost too much.

After I knocked repeatedly at the Centre's front door, several people came down and let us in. Apparently we were expected one day later and so they were surprised to see us, but they graciously took us to our little second floor apartment. It's rather nice — and it has an air-conditioner. We will need it in humid Singapore.

Today at breakfast, after chapel, and during the noon and evening meals we met a number of the students. They are quite mature. A four-year college or university degree is an admissions prerequisite. But in addition to that, most of them have already had pastoral or mission experience. Others have tentatively left previous vocations (civil engineering and computer programming, for example) and are looking toward Christian ministry. The youngest student, I was told, is 25. The Centre is interdenominational and the students come from half a dozen or eight Asian countries.

April 4

I am impressed with Dean Peskett and his wife Rozella. They are English in nationality, Anglican by profession, and have been at the Centre for 15 years. He is scholarly, practical, and gracious. He felt very bad about not meeting us last night ("just a failure in my mental processes") and apologized profusely. It seems that DTC has a long-standing tradition of rolling out a red carpet, so to speak, for incoming profs.

The Centre is on high ground. From our windows and our small balcony we can look across the green lawn and past palms, flowering trees, and red roofs to the distant skyscraper skyline. We can't get over the attractiveness and modern aura of Singapore, as compared to Rangoon — and the rich tropical greenery, as compared to the brownness and semi-aridity we saw at Pune. Rains are frequent. Located so far south that it is almost on the equator, Singapore does not have a long dry season that is broken only by annual or semiannual monsoon downpours.

April 5

An island city, a metropolis in fact, with a population of over 2½ million, Singapore is also an independent nation, a 20th century city-state and a highly efficient one. The island dimensions are 27 miles (east-west) by 14 (north-south). Modern, verdant, and scrupulously clean, Singapore is both a surprise and a delight to the Western visitor.

April 6

Here at Singapore we are only 75 miles north of the equator. Today I looked at the world map in the lobby. What lies below the equator? Only Australia, New Zealand, a portion of Africa, most of South America, part of Indonesia, and some of the South Sea Islands. Virtually nothing else — except for vast reaches of ocean. Most of terra firma lies north of the equator. The big dramatic fact about the southern half of our planet is Byron's "deep and dark blue ocean."

April 7

In a recent article on Malaysia in "The Far Eastern Economic Review," I was amazed to find that two of the 13 states of Malaysia are separated from the rest by hundreds of miles of South China Sea. While the 11 states of Malaysia proper are in the long north-south Malay Peninsula, the other two, Sabah and Sarawak, are in the northern and northwestern portions of the island of Borneo — and the entire South China Sea lies between. I thought I had a fairly good grasp of national borders; this data thoroughly surprised me.

April 10

In midafternoon I got into conversation with Abraham Tan, a student from Surabaya, East Java. He is 30, a former — and quite successful — civil engineer, and has a Chinese family background. At 20 he left his Confucian-Taoist way of life and became a Christian. He is now in the Presbyterian Church. In speaking of his conversion, he said, "I was willing to do the will of God. I wept; I confessed my sins." Presbyterian and Mennonite groups in Indonesia (and also Perkantas, the Indonesia Inter-Varsity Fellowship) have extended service invitations to him. It is no wonder; he is poised, manly, and personable.

April 11

On a trip into downtown Singapore this morning I took the wrong bus and found myself eight or ten blocks from my destination. Before hailing a taxi I spotted the most unattractive piece of architecture that has ever afflicted my eyesight, the Sri Mariamman (Hindu) Temple on South Bridge Road. The upper portion of the structure is a triangular tower heaped and piled high with polychromed Hindu deities and devotees. The architect obviously aimed at a pyramidal pattern of color, diversity, and amplitude. But he jammed together a multitude of figures in a commixture of clashing colors, and the final effect is garish and forced.

April 12

Just across the table from us this evening was Suee (Soo) Yan. He is a student from Malaysia but has lived for several years in Australia where he still has his membership in a Baptist church. His sense of isolation — he is the only Christian in a family of 11 children — has not kept him from reaching out in a warm and practical way toward his fellow-students. He is well-known for the cards of encouragement and appreciation he drops in their mailboxes. Today he said to me, "My father is not a Christian. My mother probably is; I'm not sure. She has mental problems." In a thumbnail portrait of him another student wrote, "Suee Yan's consistent and fervent prayer is for his family...to receive Christ."

April 13

On this Sunday morning we attended the large Barker Road Methodist Church. A lay brother served as worship leader. My first impression was of his fine English, but then as he prayed I became aware of his constant repetition of "Lord" and "Father." In a 10 or 15 minute prayer he used them at least 150 times.

After the choir did its best (it was none too good), the visiting preacher, a young New Zealander and dean of the Tung Ling Bible School, took charge of the service. He went immediately to the piano, caressed the keys, and informed us via the mike that he would teach us two choruses. He first crooned them for us, and then we tried to sing along with him. Oh yes, at one point we were exhorted to lift our hands in praise. He then preached enthusiastically, and not without effectiveness, on the lifted hands of Moses in Exodus 17.

Several students from the Centre were there and we walked back with them. On the way I talked with Chiu (Choo) Hea, a single woman with a Chinese background from Malacca on the west coast of Malaysia. She has just returned from Harvard with a B.A. in psychology. "I avoided B.F. Skinner's books," she told me. She has an oval, attractive face, and is very feminine. When she leaves DTC she wants to do graduate work at Syracuse University in marriage and family counseling. "I don't have the experience," she said, "but if I did, I wouldn't have the time for counseling."

We have been learning to know Darmawan and Deborah Sembiring, an Indonesian student couple from the Batak tribe, now largely Lutheran, in North Sumatra. Her mother was a nominal third generation Christian and her father an animist. Because he wanted this Christian girl, he accepted Christianity, albeit in a formal way. Later however he became more earnest about Christian experience and then led his wife into a deeper commitment.

Although Darmawan's parents were raised in animism, they and all their children joined the Dutch Reformed Church. The family members were syncretistic, however; they attended church services but they also continued to pray to animistic spirits. While Darmawan was in medical school in Java, he was influenced by a vigorous Christian student fellowship. Afterward he helped his parents find a more mature relationship with Christ.

Deborah and Darmawan met at a Jakarta church gathering. After their marriage and his graduation from medical school, they worked at jungle hospitals in West Kalimantan (part of what was once called Borneo). Now they are studying Bible and theology for two years before returning to West Kalimantan to serve in a Baptist mission hospital. They have a splendid blend of poise and high spirits. Partly no doubt because of the stigma attached to barrenness in her culture, Deborah very much wants a baby. So far however they have been unsuccessful. Today while Doris and I were chatting with them, I noticed that Darmawan is putting on weight just below the beltline. I reached over, patted his tummy lightly and said to Deborah, "He's going to have the first one." She almost cracked up.

April 15

I have been swimming daily at the Toa Payoh pool. I walk there in the hot sunlight — it's about a mile and a half — finding shade along the way from trees and buildings wherever I can. When I arrive I'm always perspired, but then the water is delightful. Since I don't want to be sweated up when I get back to the Centre, I take a taxi for the return trip.

Today, after teaching Psalms 8 and 19 (I hope the students enjoyed them as much as I did), I walked to the pool and then lay on my back in the water, looking at the stupendous cloud-towers outlined against a backdrop of blue sky.

April 18

Singapore has been called "the most prosperous city-state in the world." While I have no expertise in such matters, I think the statement may be correct.

I've tried to understand at least partially this vast prosperity. The most obvious factor is Singapore's strategic location. Situated at the southern tip of the long north-south Malay Peninsula and at the funnel-like eastern entrance of the Malacca Strait (the traditional sea passage between the Pacific and Indian oceans), Singapore with its great natural harbor is the maritime crossroads of Southeast Asia. Partly as a consequence, it is also the marketplace of the region. Tin, rubber, and rice are imported from Thailand, Malaysia, and Indonesia and then exported to scores of distant countries. From the roof of a high building near the harbor I saw over 100 ships riding at anchor.

Additional factors that help explain Singapore's wealth are its major banking institutions, its high-tech industries, and the skills and diligence of its people. Three-quarters of the population are Chinese, and the Chinese of Southeast Asia are famed, and not without reason, for their industriousness. Compared to the above points, tourism is comparatively minor but still deserves mention.

Another reason, a big one, is Singapore's Prime Minister Lee Kuan Yew. Highly educated, brilliant, hardworking, and apparently scrupulously honest, Mr. Lee has been in office continuously since 1959.

April 20

As we did a week ago, we attended church this morning at Barker Road Methodist. After a layman spoke on witnessing, a film strip was shown on the forthcoming (June 1-7) Luis Palau Singapore Evangelistic Campaign.

I keep having questions about these high-pressure events. How many of the decisions are made by unchurched people? Do the follow-up programs get most of the previously unchurched converts into congregations? Does participation in such a campaign once every two or five years give passive, quietistic church members a sense of confidence that they have thereby fulfilled their witnessing obligations to their neighbors and friends? In a big campaign, are people primarily called to confession — or are they also called to New Testament discipleship? Are community and social justice issues raised? How about the flamboyance and showmanship and cost? If Jesus was here in the flesh would He put His blessing on such efforts? Would He say, "Rebuke them not; he that is not against me is for me?"

Does an evangelistic campaign almost automatically produce a letdown when the big push is over? If so, is this simply a corollary to the mountaintop-valley emotional pattern that sometimes occurs in Christian experience? Would it not be better for congregations to engage in a combination of friendship evangelism and personal witness all the time? But since most congregations won't do this, perhaps occasional big efforts are a second-best technique. I wonder how much good they actually do. Some, I am sure — and perhaps more than I think.

Oh yes, I should add a statistic from the film strip. Twelve percent of the Singapore population is classified as Christian.

April 21
Today Doris and I went on a bus tour around the island. At one of the first stops, a garden near the Jurong Bird Park, we saw several trees that had been planted by visiting dignitaries from other countries. At the base of each was a plaque containing the name of the esteemed official and the date of the ceremony. One sign declared that Ferdinand Marcos of the Philippines had planted this particular tree in 1976. I pointed to it and proclaimed, "May no fruit grow on you forever!" However, no immediate withering was apparent.

From the garden and the Marcos tree we drove north into the less settled area of the island — past orchards, palm groves, vegetable plots, and smaller, more humble houses. After turning off the main highway onto a meandering little road we came to the north shore and looked across the Straits of Johore, here a mile wide, to the southern tip of Malaysia. Just east and west of this point, on February 8, 1942, the Japanese invaders crossed the straits in commandeered sampans and assaulted Singapore. It was the beginning of the end for this Far Eastern British bastion. Seven days later, after the Japanese had penetrated to the heart of the island, Singapore surrendered.

Later we drove past the infamous Changi Prison. Here, after the February 15 surrender, the Japanese jammed 8,000 prisoners of war into quarters originally designed for a third or a quarter that many.

At our final stop, the Crocodilarium, we saw about 100

of these armor-plated reptiles. A sign says that male crocodiles grow up to 20 feet in length, and some of those we saw surely came close to that. From the walkway above the pool I waved my hat vigorously at one directly beneath the railing, and he responded by rearing angrily upward with a mighty snapping of his jaws. Or perhaps he thought my hat was a new and fascinating fruit and he was reaching for a new taste experience.

Today our guide told us that all Singapore employees, both in government and private industry, receive only 75% of their monthly salaries. The remainder goes into an Old Age fund and is held until a person is 55. Withdrawals however can be made for either real estate or investment. The 25% is non-taxable and earns interest.

On our 75-mile tour of the island today we constantly saw vistas of trees, parks, and flowers. The credit for this must go to Prime Minister Lee who in the sixties and seventies arranged a vast planting program. "He was determined," said our guide, "that Singapore would not become another Hong Kong" — in terms of partial barrenness, that is.

Chiu Hea, the Malaysian woman student, represents an unusual combination of intellect, fluency, sensitivity, sociability, charm, dedication, and beauty. That is quite a list of words, but then she is quite a person.

One day she said to me, "At Harvard I played a guitar in the meetings of the Fellowship of Christian Athletes. They were big guys — mostly football players." As petite Chiu Hea spoke the last sentence (she is about 5'1") she raised her arms way up. I asked her if any of those Christian athletes had tried to marry her. "Not them," she replied. "But I couldn't marry an American man. And then I got back to Asia and found I couldn't marry an Asian man!"

"Couldn't" is a strong word, Chiu Hea. I am sure that various men will try to change your usage of it.

April 24

Today I talked with Peter Jamir, an Indian student. He was born into a Baptist family in Assam (northeastern India) and accepted Christ personally at 17 while he was a high school student in Nagaland, one of the Assam states.

After graduating from a Roman Catholic college in Shillong, Meghalaya — another of the Assam states — and also obtaining an M.A. at a Shillong university, Peter went to Union Biblical Seminary in Pune, India. But he was frustrated by the seminary's insistence that he take the prescribed preliminary English instruction before starting Bible and theology courses. "Even those who had won academic honors in English had to emphasize English for a term," he told me. "There was no option." He thought he had enough English, but the seminary was firm and he had to conform.

Later Peter had to face another hurdle. The seminary required him to leave the campus for a year of practical work in a church before returning for further study. If I understood him correctly, this stipulation involved everyone who had come directly from a university without a year of either church work or secular employment. Peter felt he had fulfilled this with six years of part-time work for an interdenominational group in Shillong. The seminary didn't agree however and again he had to knuckle under.

Back to Shillong Peter went. During the year of practical church work that followed, he decided to switch from Union Biblical Seminary in Pune to the Discipleship Training Centre in Singapore. "How do you feel now about your decision?" I asked him. He answered quite carefully. "There is a different atmosphere here, a different way of looking at things. At UBS study was more one-sided, more oriented to Asian concerns; here at DTC one gets a variety of viewpoints. Most of the students at UBS are Indian; DTC is very international. UBS is a larger community. One can be alone there and non-involved. DTC is smaller and has more of a family atmosphere."

Discipleship Training Centre reminds me of my beloved seminary Alma Mater, Biblical in New York City. I think of seven similarities: spiritual vitality, small size, interdenominational fellowship, family spirit, student maturity, conservatism without rigidity, and Biblicism without an insistence on a certain theory of Biblical inerrancy.

April 27

Doris and I have enjoyed a friendship with Shelley and Lewis Sung, a student couple from Taiwan. When they met in Taipei nine years ago they were attracted to each other. But Shelley's parents, who were rather formal Christians, opposed the match. In fact, they forbade it. They were afraid, and not without reason, that she and Lewis would become caught up in Christian work.

Her parents kept bringing young men to her but she didn't want any of them; she wanted Lewis. Finally her parents said, "You must wait five years." They agreed to wait, but then, as Shelley told the story to Doris, "a miracle happened." At the end of 2 ½ years her parents relented and she and Lewis were married. Then they worked together for Campus Evangelical Fellowship in Taiwan. The present year in Singapore is their first sabbatical. With them are their two delightful children, Jason (4) and Joy (2).

Lewis is earnest, disciplined, poised, and has a great sense of humor. Shelley has a warm personality; she is richly feminine.

April 28

At 1:30 we left for an afternoon bus tour to the city of Johore Bharu in extreme southern Malaysia. We crossed the Straits of Johore on the causeway. It was blown up by the British in early February 1942 as a defense measure against the Japanese army which was driving down the Malay Peninsula. The Japanese however crossed the straits in small boats and later seized the broken causeway and repaired it.

For a short distance in Johore Bharu we drove on Malaysia Route 1. This highway continues north 500 miles to the Thai border — and then within Thailand for an additional 700 miles to Bangkok. Quite briefly we visited the old royal palace grounds, the Abu Bakar Mosque, and a batik shop. Of the 15 million people in Malaysia, 56% are Muslim, 15% are Hindu, and 5% are Christian. Animism, Buddhism, Confucianism, and Taoism are also represented.

April 29

In the current issue of "The Far Eastern Economic Review" a writer quotes an unmarried tourist lady who was flying recently on CAAC, the Chinese national airline. As she watched the plane's video screen she was suddenly brought to full alert. "Imagine my feelings," she said, "as we were informed, by syllables flashing one after the other on the screen, that what we were about to see was an...'Inflight Annunciation!'"

April 30

This evening at a Chinese restaurant Andrew and Grace Narn, a South Korean student couple, told us about their lives and Christian service patterns.

Andrew's parents were Buddhist-Confucian-Taoist. Of the seven children Andrew is the oldest, and he was the first to become a Christian. Now all seven are Christian. "When I began attending church while I was in high school, my parents were so upset. My father beat me and said 'You are not my son.' And my grandfather was even more bitter against me." Although Andrew's father now attends a church he is uncertain about Christianity. "Some time ago," Andrew said, "he was confused by a charismatic evangelist with a message of healing and success. 'It's nothing new,' my father said. 'It's just like my old religion.'"

Grace came from a strong Buddhist family. When her

grandmother became interested in Christianity, she felt that because of her husband she could not accept Christ. Then after her husband died, she became a Christian.

Before Grace and Andrew were married, her father said to him, "I don't like your profession of Christian work. Could you change it?" Andrew of course replied in the negative. "My father still allowed us to marry," said Grace. "He really likes Andrew and is more open to Christianity than he was."

Andrew and Grace are the parents of Ko-en, a marvelously keen little girl of two. She looks at one with a level, unblinking gaze, and behind those bright observant eyes seem to lie unfathomable riches. She constantly astonishes with her ever-expanding vocabulary and repertoire of songs.

Grace has been a school teacher and Andrew has served on the InterVarsity staff in Seoul. When he returns to Korea he will be in charge of training new staff members.

Michael and Beauty Adhikari are students from Bangladesh. With them are their little daughters, Lisa and Lipa. For 12 years Michael worked with New Life, a Swedish-sponsored mission in Bangladesh, and he will continue his work there when he completes his studies at DTC.

In a little biographical sketch a fellow-student said of Beauty, "She is often found in the kitchen, practising her English with Mama Lee, the cook. . . .What she has learned at DTC about community living she hopes to apply back in Bangladesh by encouraging the poor to form communities for support and cooperation. She also desires to encourage Christian wives there to be more deeply involved in their husbands' ministries."

May 3

"My parents were Buddhist-Confucian-Taoist." Several times while speaking to Christians of Chinese origin I have heard this.

What is the basis of this multiple religious

phenomenon? China never had a tradition of one dominating religion. In Confucianism, which came on the scene about 500 B.C., people found an ethical system for the management of society and the state. But the teachings of Confucius said nothing about life after death. This need was met in some degree by a form of Buddhism which promised salvation in a heavenly milieu, "the Western Paradise." And Taoism, which was even older than Confucianism, taught people to abjure striving, to engage in mystical contemplation, and to live in harmony with nature. In a mix of these three traditions the Chinese people found their religious roots.

When Doris and I realized we would spend several weeks in Singapore, we decided that while there we would visit the grave of Marion Nafziger.

We knew Marion at Eastern Mennonite College in the early 1940s. She was a Christian college student — vibrant, wholesome, committed to Christ. Years later we heard that in 1946 on her way to India for the Mennonite Central Committee she had become ill on shipboard while crossing the Pacific. She had been taken ashore at Singapore, had survived for a time, and then quite suddenly had passed away. In this way she had joined the numberless host of Revelation 7:9-17 who have given their lives for Christ.

This morning Howard Peskett, Doris, and I drove to the Bididari Cemetery to look for Marion's grave. We had the plot number; at my request the MCC at Akron, Pa., had sent it to us. Seemingly with the aid of the cemetery office and its records and maps, the grave should have been easy to find. But Bididari is vast and parts of it are overgrown. It was only after an hour of searching and with the aid of several employees that we found it.

The stone is well preserved and the grass had been cut recently. While I took photographs, Doris copied the inscription.

MARION ELIZABETH NAFZIGER. R.N.
WATERLOO, ONTARIO
CANADA
AUGUST 10, 1921 - JULY 8, 1946
RELIEF WORKER ENROUTE TO INDIA
UNDER APPOINTMENT BY THE
MENNONITE CENTRAL COMMITTEE
AKRON, PENNSYLVANIA
U.S.A.
REVELATION 14:13

Just to the east is a copse of green trees and off to the
south in the haze are the high rises and towers of central
Singapore. As we stood there, I was moved to tears. We
bowed our heads for a minute of silence and I thanked
God for Marion. I have a vivid memory of her standing
up in the old chapel at the south end of the EMC Ad
Building (it's gone now, too) giving her testimony for
Christ in an open meeting.

Tonight I read Revelation 14:13. "And I heard a voice
from heaven saying, 'Write this: Blessed are the dead
who die in the Lord henceforth.' 'Blessed indeed,' says
the Spirit, 'that they may rest from their labors, for their
deeds follow them!'"

As we were looking for her grave, and uncertain as to
whether we would find it, I said with a lump in my throat,
"Jesus will be able to find her — in the resurrection."

May 4
With brilliant bolts of lightning and diapasons of
thunder, a massive thunder-storm swept over Singapore
this afternoon. Rain fell in torrents. I had no access to a
rain gauge, but I'm sure that in 30 minutes two to three
inches came down. And I was out in it, trying to keep an
appointment at a dentist's office. For nearly half an hour
I tried in vain to hail a taxi. Part of the time I was under
shelter and part of the time I wasn't. I got soaked. Gutters

overflowed and some streets became baby rivers. Finally I found a taxi and arrived at the office only ten minutes late.

Back at the Centre after changing into dry clothing, I asked Howard if this wasn't an unusual rain, even for Singapore. "Oh no," he answered very casually.

This morning I had asked him if there is much variation in the temperature from one season to another. "No," he said. "It might be a degree or two cooler in December."

I remember a conversation on a plane several months ago with an American businessman who was returning to his Singapore firm. "I'd love to have the job of being the Singapore weather forecaster," he said. "You could say the same thing every day." Apparently the only variation in weather patterns is that it rains a little more between November and February than it does the rest of the year.

May 6

This evening, our last in Singapore, a banquet was held here at DTC in our honor. Howard spoke words of appreciation, students gave me a big poster-card with personal notes, and DTC gave us a pewter vase with an engraved inscription. After I spoke briefly, we gave Holy Land bookmarkers to the students and little trucks and dolls to their children. "A good time was had by all."

The faculty and students have been most gracious and we have learned much. Tomorrow we fly to Jakarta and Semarang on Java to begin our five weeks in Indonesia.

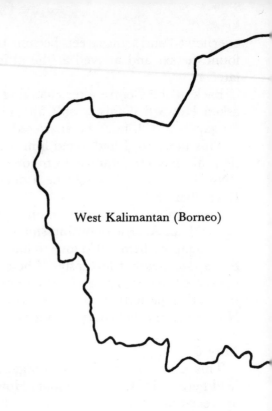

West Kalimantan (Borneo)

Jakarta

Bogor

West Java

Central
Java

Jepara

Kudus

Mt. Merapi

Borobudur

Mt. Muria

Pati

Surabaya

East Java

Java

Five Weeks
In Indonesia

Astride the equator and reaching as far east-west as from Bermuda to California, the island nation of Indonesia is a point of convergence for the Pacific and Indian Oceans and a land bridge between Australia and Asia. I had always wanted to see its tropical beauty and to visit its two Mennonite churches.

We were at Kudus, Central Java, for the first half of our stay. Then we went to Jakarta in West Java for the second half. During our stay in Kudus we visited with Charles and Lisa Christano, worked with them in their churches, and traveled over wide areas of East and Central Java. In Jakarta we spoke to church groups, to the World Vision staff, and to InterVarsity students. We also found time to see nearby verdant Bogor and the tea plantations in the hills.

May 7

I have read that Indonesia has 13,677 islands, and as our flight from Singapore to Jakarta skirted the coastline of Sumatra, we saw a large number of them.

Inasmuch as we crossed the equator today, Doris and I are now "down under," though not of course in the special Australian sense.

When we passed over the Java coastline on our approach to Jakarta we saw rice paddies of brilliant green interspersed with clusters of tall palms and red-tiled roofs. Here rice is king. "In most of Indonesia, life revolves around rice. Four out of five Indonesians work ricefields" (Bill Dalton, *Indonesia Handbook*).

I got Dalton's handbook in Singapore. At one of the Indonesian offices there I asked for a recommendation on a good book about Indonesia, and a candid, intelligent lady said, "Dalton's — but you can't take it into the country."

"Why not?" I asked in some astonishment.

"Because of a section on government corruption," she replied forthrightly. "But," she continued, "you could always cut out those pages."

On our Garuda Airways flight from Jakarta to Semarang, 300 miles east in Central Java, we read in a Jakarta newspaper that the annual Muslim fast of Ramadan would begin May 10, and that the paper would not be published May 8 "for observing the Ascension of Jesus Christ." While Islam is the predominant religion (about 85% of the people are Muslim), a robust Christian church that wields an influence out of all proportion to its size now accounts for 8 to 10% of the population. Smaller groups of Hindus and Buddhists also exist.

Lisa Christano and a small group of her friends met us at the Semarang airport (Charles was away on a preaching trip). Doris and I at last are seeing the fulfillment of the invitation given us by Charles and Lisa two years ago to visit Indonesia.

On the 30-mile drive northeast to the city of Kudus we

drove past rice fields of green and brown, and along canals where in the late afternoon heat brown-skinned people were bathing. Bicyclists with ungainly loads maneuvered at the edge of the highway, and water buffalo marched slowly and determinedly along the canal banks.

We went in the evening to a family thanksgiving service for a newborn child. To accommodate part of the large crowd, chairs had been set up outside, and we would have liked to sit there in the slight breeze and partial coolness, but since we were honored guests we were ushered into a warm inner room. The service consisted of hymns, prayers, and a message. All was in Bahasa Indonesia, the country's official language. At one point I found myself humming the familiar tune to "Holy, Holy, Holy," but the printed Bahasa words on the hymn sheet in front of me were "Kudus, Kudus, Kudus." That is how I discovered that Kudus means holy.

May 8

This morning splendid singing rang out in the Ascension Day service in Charles' church. "The Gloria Patri," "I Love to Tell the Story," and "The Doxology." All of course were sung in Bahasa Indonesia.

In spite of the heat I walked in the narrow lanes and streets near the Christano home. The close-packed neat little houses are made of cement, plaster, and brick. Tall banana trees, providing both shade and fruit, grow in profusion. The yards are of bare brown ground, but almost invariably the earthen surface has been swept clean.

Kudus is hot. Most of Indonesia is hot. Only at elevations of 3000 feet or higher does one find a cool, comfortable climate. Dalton says, "This country has a typical equatorial climate with only two seasons: the wet season and the hot season. The hot season is slightly hotter and not quite so wet as the wet season, while the wet season is slightly wetter and not quite so hot as the hot season."

Just before lunch Charles returned. We hadn't seen

him since August 11, 1984 when we said good-bye to him and Lisa in Tel Aviv. Early the next day we had flown to New York and they had prepared for their flight to Singapore and Java.

Charles Christano has had an extraordinary life. After studying in Jakarta and Singapore he became a leader in one of the Indonesia Mennonite churches. From 1978-1984 he was President of Mennonite World Conference. He has traveled in Africa, the Middle East, Russia, East Germany, the Caribbean, and North and South America. He was robbed in Bangladesh, and in his own country he has been repeatedly threatened by angry, aggressive individuals. At least twice he has talked and walked his way out of seemingly impossible situations. It is easy to think of him when one reads Paul's chronicle of hardships in II Corinthians 11.

May 9
This afternoon Charles took us to the Great Mosque of Kudus. The earliest of its three towers dates to the 16th century, and it was here in Kudus that the first Muslim Kingdom of Java was founded. As we walked about the mosque area, we received courteous treatment from the Muslim officials.

Some thought has been given to the possibility of a short trip by Charles, Doris, and me to West Kalimantan (what once was called Borneo). Deep in the interior at Putussibau Charles' church has begun a mission outreach. Now 13 congregations have been established within the area. This is where Luke and Dorothy Beidler and Paul and Esther Bucher (all from eastern Pennsylvania) served for several years as Mennonite missionaries with Charles' church group, and I had expressed an interest in going there for a visit. But last night when Charles met with his elders the decision was negative. I understand; there is simply not enough time within the 34 Indonesian days at our disposal.

Dorothy Beidler has written beautifully in the

September 1984 "Missionary Messenger" about Inai Kinta, a young Kantú woman of Putussibau who became a Christian. What does this new relationship to Christ mean to her, Dorothy asks. "Does she consciously exult in being a daughter of the Lord? Does she sit in quiet meditation...?"

"I think the answer is 'no.' Inai Kinta is not the product of Western experiential spirituality as I am. She has come out of an animistic religious tradition where God the Creator was unattainable and the lesser spirits which related to humankind were to be entreated or tricked into benevolence through carrying out prescribed rituals. But now Inai Kinta is a Christian. What does this mean for her?

"In the beginning it was a matter of simple belief. . . . The picture of Jesus nailed to the cross, a human sacrifice of the highest order, moved her. Jesus gave himself as a sacrifice in the tradition of Kantú animal sacrifices, and this was new and amazing. This giving of his life is the basis for forgiveness of sins. Inai Kinta wanted to have this forgiveness and the salvation she sees symbolized by the baptism certificate that she has carefully stored away.

"Perhaps this is all Inai Kinta wanted and expected on the day of her baptism. But God had and continues to have much more to give her. And this is the mystery — God is giving and Inai Kinta is receiving."

May 11
On this Sunday morning I spoke in two churches (at 6:00 and 7:30 a.m.) It seems there are two reasons for the early services: first, to beat the heat, and second, to have the rest of the day free. Charles said to me, "Now don't go home and tell your friends that Charles Christano has his people so spiritual that they get up for 6:00 a.m. services."

May 12
Today I browsed in Charles' library. It is very broad; it

deals with many subjects. A broad-gauge man will have a many-faceted library. Lisa says, "Every time he comes home from a trip he brings books and books." In room after room he has them lined up and stored and stashed. I admit he could use the library organizational skills of a Rosemary Wyse. But so could I.

I am beginning to learn about the two Mennonite churches in Indonesia. They bear the initials GITJ and GKMI.

The Evangelical Church of Java (Gereja Injili di Tanah Jawa — thus GITJ) is the primary result of the first modern Mennonite foreign mission. In the middle of the 19th century the Dutch Mennonites, later assisted by German and Russian Mennos, began a work near Mt. Muria on the northern coast of Central Java. This outreach was called the Mennonite Mission.

The church grew over the decades but between 1942 and 1949 it was almost destroyed. During World War II, the occupying Japanese tortured and killed. And some local Javanese took advantage of the chaotic era to harass the church. Then during the '45-49 war of independence, fought by Javanese patriots against their Dutch masters who had returned in '45 when the Japanese withdrew, the Muria area was overrun and heavily damaged by the Dutch. By 1949, the year of Indonesian independence, membership was down to a mere 1,000. Since that time it has risen to about 45,000 — and some put the figure higher. Exact numbers are unobtainable.

Pak Joyo, as he is affectionately called, was one of the reasons for the resurgence. "Joyo" is an abbreviation of his much longer actual name, and "Pak" comes from the Indonesian word for "father" or "papa." Pak Joyo was greatly gifted both as a preacher and as an administrator. After nearly forty years of excellent leadership he is now in retirement. Paulus Sutartono is currently the official head, and Soesanto Harso is the General Secretary.

The church is still growing rapidly. While this growth is partly traceable to the ethnic identity of the Javanese

GITJ membership and the Javanese village folk of the Muria area, a strong pattern of friendship evangelism has also contributed greatly.

Poverty is a major problem. The church has insufficient resources for education and building. Each year the Mennonite Central Committee contributes to the church general fund and also to several commissions.

The GITJ is rural and congregation-oriented. Lay leadership is prominent. Javanese music, arts, and crafts flourish among its people. The church is still highly localized in the Muria region; a circle 45 miles in diameter would cover nearly all its locations.

Only recently has the GITJ begun establishing church groups on Sulawesi (Celebes), Kalimantan (Borneo), and Sumatra. These groups are basically GITJ members from Java who have been resettled by the government. A massive effort, it should be said, is being made by Indonesia to transplant people from overpopulated Java to the more open terrain of the other major islands. The MCC is assisting the people and the government in this program.

The story of what is today the Muria Christian Church of Indonesia (Gereja Kristen Muria Indonesia — thus GKMI) began in about 1917 when Tee Siem Tat, a successful Chinese businessman in Kudus, sought healing through a Salvation Army leader. While no dramatic healing occurred, Tee's health slowly improved, and meanwhile Tee and his family and friends were receiving Christian teaching from Lieutenant Tanuhatu, the Salvation Army officer. Tee's conversion took place in 1918 or 1919 and he then requested baptism. The Salvation Army however does not engage in baptism, and Tee looked elsewhere, first to the Adventists and then to an independent mission (with Lutheran and Reformed elements) at Salatiga. Tee was not satisfied with the full pattern of doctrines and practices of either the Adventists or the Salatiga group, and finally on December 6, 1920, he and his wife and a circle of Chinese relatives and friends were baptized by missionaries of the Mennonite Mission. This baptismal service, in a sense, was the beginning of the GKMI church.

The Chinese group in Kudus developed unusual spiritual warmth, vitality, and power. Within three years a missionary said of them, "This congregation really reminds us of the church in Jerusalem." Under Tee's leadership the group witnessed and led others to Christ and into the experience of baptism. By 1927 the Kudus congregation was independent, and although it expressed a desire to continue its relationship with the Mennonite Mission, it was well on the way to becoming a second Mennonite denomination in Indonesia.

For several decades the GKMI, as it finally came to be called, did not emphasize its early Mennonite connection. But in later years it affiliated with Mennonite World Conference.

Much of its early growth came from evangelism among the Chinese segment of the Muria population, but then it began leaping its ethnic frontier. What had begun as a small Chinese congregation in Kudus became a church of over 7,000 members, with both city and rural locations. MCC funds have helped in this expansion. Congregations have been established in the jungles of Java, Sumatra, and West Kalimantan, and also in major cities. In the capital city of Jakarta alone it now has ten congregations. It is a vigorous, well-organized church. A number of its members are well-to-do, if not wealthy, and its leadership is unusually well trained. It is an exciting church. And Charles Christano is one of its exciting leaders.

May 13

Early this morning the Christanos and Doris and I drove 35 miles to Bandengan Beach on the Java Sea. As the road wound through forested areas we saw many lightly constructed, neat frame houses (the color of light coffee) nestled beneath teakwood, kapok, mahogany, and chico trees. The houses were open and airy and had lattices for shade.

In a village through which we passed, many Christians had been killed in the early 1940s — killed by Javanese with the encouragement of the occupying Japanese. Some Chinese parents in this area hid their daughters for years, lest the girls be forced into prostitution in Japanese military camps. Gentle, sweet-spirited Lisa Christano spoke with animation of Japanese cruelty during World War II.

At the beach I saw just offshore a double-sailed *perahu*. In the Gulf of Aden it would be called a *dhow* (the Arabic word).

Charles Christano's Chinese name was Tan Ing Tjioe. He told me today that his new name includes "Christ," his former name "Tan," and the suffix "no" from "cino," a Javanese word which means "Chinese." "A loose translation of Christano," he said, "would be 'The ex-Chinese who was Tan belongs to Christ.'"

May 14

Today I leafed through the Christano guest book. One of their guests wrote, "If 'joy is the most infallible sign of the presence of God,' God is in your place." And opposite our names I wrote this: "Our times of sharing have been precious to us. You give us new hope in the progress of God's Kingdom."

May 15

In the Holy Land in '84, while Charles, Lisa, Doris, and I were seated at a kibbutz restaurant table in the Jezreel Valley, he told us of a miraculous healing in which he was involved. Today, in response to a question, he told me more.

Some years ago Charles received a message from a Javanese woman in a distant village. Incidentally, the woman was not a Christian but an adherent of another religion. "Come," she said. "Heal my daughter. She is blind." Charles was taken aback. "I'm no healer," he told me. "That has not been my gift. But I knew I had to go. So I took three friends and we started off. All the way we prayed and prayed. The closer we got the more certain we were that God was going to do something. When we approached the house we saw crowds of people around it. They knew we were coming, and they wanted to know what was going to happen.

"We went in and found a lovely young woman in her late teens. We knelt, laid our hands on her head, and prayed. And she opened her eyes! God had healed her! Impulsively she reached out to give me a hug of thanks and joy, but then in maidenly modesty drew back.

"As a result of her healing the young woman became a Christian. A few days later her blindness returned and she sent for me to come again. 'No,' I said, 'you're a Christian now; you can pray for your own healing.' She did so and her sight was restored a second time. Now she has full sight and is a Christian wife and mother."

May 16

While we were discussing marriage issues, Charles asked me, "What should we do if a man with three wives becomes a Christian and wants baptism?" Then he answered his own question. "We study each case separately. We look at such factors as the age of the wives, the number and ages of the children, the feeling of the other wives about the Christian faith, and the possibility of remarriage for the wives. Sometimes we allow the man to stay with the three wives if they are old and have no possibility of remarriage.

"Some have said to me, 'You are too loose; you are encouraging polygamy.' I have answered that there were probably multiple marriages in the Early Church, for a church leader was to be 'the husband of one wife.'"

Then he turned to the issue of praying for the dead. "It is Javanese custom," Charles said, "to have prayers for the dead on the 3rd, 40th, 100th, and 1,000th day after death. We teach that we should not pray for the dead; we use the story in Luke 16. We don't believe in a second chance after death. For the sake however of maintaining contact with Javanese relatives, we have Bible reading, singing, evangelistic speaking, and the giving of thanks for the one who has gone on before.

"We need indigenization; we need contextualization. But where does contextualization end and compromise begin? We must be careful; we don't want to baptize idolatry."

In the evening Charles, Lisa, and Doris and I drove 35 miles northwest to Jepara where Charles spoke in the GITJ congregation of Paulus Sutartono. Even though I don't understand Indonesian, the service was impressive. I heard enthusiastic, full-volume singing by the hundreds who were present. They really pounded it out. Paulus himself was the dynamic song leader. Then after two numbers by a youth singing group, Charles, at the special request of Paulus, gave the first segment of a two-part message on stewardship and tithing. I wish I could have understood Charles. He spoke with strength and fluency, and his audience was obviously with him. I saw intense rapt faces and heard appreciative chuckles. I turned and whispered to Doris, "He's a man of destiny."

May 18

Traveling in a rented van with a driver, seven of us left this morning for a three-day trip through portions of Central and East Java. The seven: Charles, Lisa, their three children (Stephen, Philip, and Fiona), and Doris and I.

We went south through Semarang, Ungaran, and Ambarawa. At noon we came to Borobudur, the great eighth century Javanese Buddhist stupa, a "colossal man-made cosmic mountain" (Dalton). Dalton says further, "Built with more than two million cubic feet of stone, it's...the largest ancient monument in the southern hemisphere." Somehow I didn't like it. It's enormous, yes, and a tribute to its determined builders, but it's squat and made of black volcanic stones. It looks a bit like a gigantic tortoise that could crawl no further and expired. I thought of J. Lankester Harding's words about Petra in *The Antiquities of Jordan*. "Petra is one of those places which you find either incredibly attractive...or depressing and sinister. . . .But whether you like or dislike it, it is one of those places which should be seen, for there is nothing else like it in the world."

We stopped for the night at a guest house on the southern slope of Mt. Merapi, a volcano famed for both beauty and vigor. In a way that volcanoes have, it blew part of its conical tip skyward a half century ago.

Just before dusk several of us swam in a pool at the base of a verdant, nearly vertical cliff. The water was colder than I thought water could be in Indonesia. However, we are at 3,300 feet.

Today we saw tropical verdure, high peaks, tiers of rice fields, patient bullocks, bicycles with almost impossible loads, old women with bulky burdens, dense bamboo clusters, intriguing little shaded roads I would have liked to investigate, marvelously persistent but unfailingly courteous vendors, and crotchety tourists — and, oh yes, the conical hats that shade the faces of bent-over ricefield workers.

May 19

In early morning five of us (Charles, his two boys, and Doris and I) hiked partway up the heavily wooded flank of Mt. Merapi. The trail, or rather the almost endless sequences of crude stone steps, led steeply upward around bend after bend in the dense shade of great trees. After two hours we came out onto the ridge, and there just ahead was the splendid peak and steaming crater of Merapi. We rested and took pictures. "How far to the top?" I asked Charles.

"About three miles," he answered. "And it would be five hours up and three down."

I looked longingly, but I knew we didn't have the extra

eight hours. "Maybe next time," I said to myself, and then we turned and started down.

Today we drove south and then northeast and finally east. In Yogyakarta, a university town, it was Commencement Day, and vast numbers of graduates (in academic attire) and their families were strolling on the sidewalks. Later we stopped at Prambanan, an 11th century Hindu temple. It was another ancient edifice of black stones; it didn't speak to me. Afterward we drove through Solo, "the cradle of Javanese culture," and then turned east and began climbing into the high hill country. Just before dusk we visited Sukuh, another Hindu temple, and a few of us saw its erotic sculptures. But they were quite paltry compared to the opulent forms and astonishing frankness of Khajuraho in India.

Near the East Java boundary we rented a mountain villa and ate the evening meal in our big central dining room. Charles and Lisa are great hosts and traveling companions. This is the way to see Java.

May 20

On the way to the ridge crest, the boundary between Central and East Java, we saw marvellous rice terraces — green velvet stairways ascending the hill slopes. Since this is National Remembrance Day (one way to put it into English), Indonesia flags are lining the roads. As we went down, down, down from the cool mountains into East Java and the heat, Charles told us why this is a special day. A group of Indonesian students met on this date in 1908 and began planning for an independent nation. The Dutch were not pleased. Some of the students were arrested and imprisoned and the movement was suppressed.

While the Netherlands today is a progressive, liberal, humanitarian nation, the Dutch were rapacious and exploitative in their East Indies colonial domain. They rigged the economic balances quite thoroughly in favor of themselves, denied dissent, and withheld educational opportunities from most of their benighted subjects. Here is an illustration of the last point: in 1940, only two years before the Japanese threw out the Dutch, 90% of the native population was illiterate, and far less than 1,000 Indonesians — out of a population of 68 million — had high school diplomas.

We drove for a time through extensive teakwood forests. Teak is a magnificent hardwood and all teak trees are under state control. At Cepu we crossed back into Central Java and arrived at Kudus in mid-afternoon.

May 21

Today four pastors and businessmen took Doris and me 70 miles southeast to a Javanese jungle village where the GKMI has a new congregation. Our car had a powerful engine and all its power was needed; the last two miles constituted a driving adventure. The road, narrow and rocky, wound through a dense forest and up and down steep slopes. At one point we had to get out and push.

An excited band of little children, some of them as bare as Adam and Eve, came running when they heard the car. Few older children, young people, or adults were present. Most of them were away at school, a long walk on jungle paths, or working in the fields. Rice, custard-apples, cassava, and sweet potatoes are grown.

Poised and gracious, the young mothers and the older people made us welcome. In response to a written invitation by a number of the villagers, the GKMI has been working here for 2 ½ years. Now there are over 200 members, and they have their own Javanese pastor. The people were left under no illusions that their way would be easy. "You may be persecuted," they were told. "Becoming a Christian disciple can be costly." But the word of truth had fallen on good ground, and now there is a continuing harvest.

Miracles have played a part in the growth of the village church. When local medicine men and doctors sometimes couldn't help, pastors and their people prayed for the healing of friends, and miracles happened.

After preaching the Gospel and gaining adherents, the GKMI began assisting in literacy, education, and health. A GKMI pastor said to me, "We believe in evangelism first — and *then* social work.

In the village today I saw a confirmation of what I have been learning and sensing: the GKMI has not allowed itself to be confined to its Chinese ethnic origins, but like the first century church in Jerusalem has leaped across cultural barriers to serve a larger world.

Today I also learned that the GKMI procedure is to send out promising men as evangelists, and then if they are faithful to ordain them as pastors.

May 23

Early this morning Paulus Sutartono drove down from Jepara, picked up Doris and me, and drove us to the GITJ synod office in Pati, 15 miles east of Kudus. There we met Soesanto Harso, General Secretary of the synod, a highly personable individual — "a Javanese gentleman," as Charles Christano described him.

Soesanto was quite helpful; he gave us much data on the GITJ: its school at Pati, its involvement in the resettlement program, and its congregations. When he referred however to the locations of two large congregations as 15 and 20 kilometers "west of Jepara," I was confused. Jepara is on the coast, and west of that city is only the Java Sea. Those two churches are really in deep water! But perhaps there was more of a language barrier than I thought. Or perhaps the four directions are used far less in Indonesia than in our American midwest.

Paulus then took us around the adjacent AKWW campus. The school has an excellent name: Akademi Kristen Wiyata Wacana (The Disciple of the Word Christian Academy).

May 24

Charles Christano is a remarkable man. He has the

drive of a Japanese export firm salesman, the instincts of a corporation lawyer, the organizational skills of a Harvard Business School graduate, the boldness of an Old Testament prophet, a goodly measure of the spirit of Jesus, a special endowment of the Holy Spirit, a gift for counseling, a vigorous platform manner, and a vast confidence in prayer. Not to mention a zest for life and a rich sense of humor. He also has a strong ego — not a negative thing in itself. In fact, it is an almost inevitable concomitant of dynamic leadership. But it can get away from him and lead him to expatiate over-long in a highly opinionated way when something rankles him. Lisa, I believe, is aware of this and is a gentle moderating influence.

One day I said, "Charles, you drive a car like I used to. I gave nervous breakdowns to a whole squadron of guardian angels."

May 25

In a Cantonese restaurant in Semarang today, just before our takeoff for Jakarta, I had my first encounter with fried dove. I think it should have been freed for a life on the wing. It had very little flesh. Its tiny little legs were like overgrown toothpicks.

At the airport we said good-bye to Charles and Lisa Christano. We enjoyed greatly our visit in their home — and our work and travel experiences with them. May God bless and protect them.

We arrived in early evening at Allen Harder's Mennonite Central Committee house in Jakarta. Although Allen is away on an MCC trip to Sulawesi (Celebes), his housekeeper is efficiently meeting our needs. After dinner I walked for a half hour in the moonlight along residential streets. It was a warm evening. At one point I passed a mosque where in a large room an immense number of women, heavily veiled in white, were kneeling in worship. In an adjacent room a lesser number of men were kneeling. Apparently it was an evening Ramadan service.

May 26

We slept more or less successfully for eight hours in spite of a miscellany of noise: motorcycles, bemos (three-wheelers), taxis, trucks (mufflers seem to be forbidden here), tropical birds, goats, insomnious roosters, the insistent tattoos of Ramadan food vendors, and the high-decibel 4:00 a.m. intrusion from the nearby mosque.

May 28

On this hot day we visited the National Monument. Its carefully designed fluted shaft rises 350 feet. From the top we surveyed the juxtaposed old and modern structures of this sprawling major city (population: 7 million), Indonesia's capital. Contrasts abound: skyscrapers and slums, high rises and hovels, glitter and degradation, plutocrats and paupers. But this is not the whole picture. Large numbers in the city live within a sturdy and comfortable middle class.

Along the four walls of the enormous concourse beneath the Monument are tableaux depicting Indonesia's colorful history. I enjoyed them.

In spite of the heat, and largely because of a skillful interpreter, the Middle East lecture in the GKMI church in West Jakarta went very well this evening. Last night it was different. A gracious lady — a young Christian, I was told — tried to serve as interpreter, but was unable to do direct verbal translation beyond the fourth or fifth grade level. I never geared down so far or struggled so hard for communication in my life. Much of the time toward the end I was reduced to saying a short clause or phrase or three or four words at a time. It was a hot night and by the close of the session I could have wrung water out of my shirt.

May 29

The Muslim month of Ramadan has now been underway for 19 days. One of the five pillars or key requirements of Islam, it is the sacred month of the Muslim calendar.

During Ramadan an observant Muslim is obliged to fast each day from dawn — as soon as one can distinguish between a white thread and a black one — until sunset. No food or drink can be taken. Smoking and sexual intercourse are also prohibited. In its most rigid formulation, one cannot even swallow his own saliva. Exemptions are granted to soldiers, travelers, the sick, the elderly, and menstruating, pregnant, or nursing women.

Ramadan is designed as a time of spiritual discipline, a time to combat self-indulgence. It is a special month of both worship and charity. But in hot tropical countries in the summertime and especially when one attempts to carry out a full program of daily labor without any food or water, the physical and emotional demands are enormous.

Since the Muslim calendar is lunar and has only 354 days, the month of Ramadan "works its way around" our calendar. For example, in 1975 when we were in Egypt, Ramadan was in September. This year it began May 10. In another decade it will fall in midwinter. I once had the irreverent thought that if a loyal Muslim living in Thule, Greenland, where the summer sun doesn't set for weeks at a time, would encounter a midsummer Ramadan, he would die of starvation. I've discovered however that Islamic thought is not unaware of this problem and that one solution for the faithful is to observe the fast only in terms of the hours of daylight at the 45th parallel.

Ramadan obviously has positive elements. In actual practice however, from what I've seen in Cairo and here, the emphasis is more on the night-time feasting than the daylight fasting.

May 30

This morning friends took us to visit Miniature Indonesia on the south side of Jakarta. It's the Smithsonian, the National Cathedral, Radio City Music Hall, and

Disneyland rolled into one. Built on a vast scale and with seeming disregard for cost, it is a celebration of the cultural and religious diversity among the island peoples, an assertion of national unity, and a locale for spectacle and entertainment. It has an imposing structure for each of the main areas and religions of the land, an impressive reception hall for visiting dignitaries, a modern theater for cultural programs, a state-of-the-art super-screen cinema, and a major museum. And from an aerial tramway one can look down on green grassy islands (located in a large lagoon) that are placed and shaped to represent all the major islands of the Indonesian archipelago. Miniature Indonesia, indeed!

May 31

Today, from a quiet, respected Christian worker who is visiting in Jakarta, I heard the story of an almost incredible event. It happened in the Javanese back country in 1969 or 1970. As the story was being told, I took notes and then later read the full account to my source. "Yes," he said, "you have it right."

A simple pastor (I will call him Anwar), never officially ordained and without any theological training, was struggling amid conditions of poverty and near-famine to lead his people. In this difficult time, a poor Javanese Christian couple and their two-year-old daughter came to stay with the pastor and his wife (I'll call her Wati). Since the little girl was the couple's only surviving child she was especially precious. But she became ill and because there was no money in the house, she could not be taken to a doctor or a hospital. Every day she became worse.

Anwar and Wati and the child's parents could do nothing but pray. Anwar expected God's miracle to heal the child, but she became weaker and weaker. Anwar and his wife cried with the parents. They all prayed intensely. They placed the little girl in God's hands, but her condition grew worse. She was dying. The parents and the pastor and his wife continued to cry and pray. Then something happened. The child began to revive.

For Anwar it was a traumatic experience. His faith was strengthened. The parents and the pastor couple praised God. The happiness of the four adults however didn't last long. Two weeks later the little girl died. The seeming healing had been wonderful, but the death left them dumbfounded.

Sadly Anwar went to the local officials to arrange for burial in the village cemetery. The death was the first in his congregation; he did not know there would be a problem concerning burial arrangements. But there was. "This is a Muslim cemetery," he was told. "Christian burials cannot be held here." Anwar was astonished. He then went to a second cemetery and again was refused. The little girl was finally buried in a Christian cemetery several miles away, a long march for the mourners in the heat and humidity and a sad location for the parents who wanted their dead nearby.

This death was only the first of many in Anwar's congregation during a two-year period. Again and again he requested burial privileges in the local cemetery. Each time he was refused. Eight times in less than two years his people had to march to the distant Christian cemetery. Anwar's indignation grew.

Then another destitute Christian couple availed themselves of the hospitality offered by Anwar and his wife. The new arrivals had a son, eleven years old, an only son. And he died. The parents and the pastor couple were prostrated with grief. Again Anwar had to face the problem of burial.

Always at the village cemetery the answer had been "No," but now the pastor had had enough. He was determined to get a local burial. Carrying the dead boy and accompanied by a crowd of villagers, some sympathetic, some hostile, some merely curious, he marched to the cemetery. There he was refused again. He felt desperate, and suddenly decided, "God will do a miracle." Crying, he embraced the boy tightly. It was already three hours after death. In anger and frustration Anwar opened his mouth to pray — and then the miracle happened. Many saw it. The boy opened his eyes. When he saw that he was being held by the pastor and not by his father, he cried out loudly, wriggled free of the pastor's arms, and ran about looking for his parents until he found them. He ran into their arms. Witnesses burst into tears. People stood in consternation and awe.

The boy, I was told, recovered completely and is living today in East Java. He is married and a Christian.

Could I convince a convention of doctors that the boy had been medically, clinically dead? No. I wouldn't try. But his parents, the pastor, and the whole village had no doubts on the subject.

Apparently in Indonesia a few such resurrection events have occurred, but I did not hear anyone say that this is typical in the life of Indonesian churches, or that such a thing will inevitably happen if one asks and has faith and has no hidden sin. Miracles of healing have also taken place, but again, I did not hear of Indonesian Christians insisting that God do their bidding.

My own view is that no passage in the Bible absolutely promises a healing event to those who ask. Not even Matthew 8:17 guarantees this. It does not say that since Jesus bore our diseases on the cross we may ask for healing and automatically receive it. It simply says that Jesus fulfilled the Old Testament prediction that Messiah would come with healing. We cannot interpret a given verse in a certain way and then demand healing. We ask; He grants, if that is His holy will. If we could always work our wills in such matters, we would be God instead of He.

June 1

This morning breakfast was at 6:00, and soon afterward a driver from World Vision came for us. I was to speak to the Jakarta staff during its chapel period. In compliance with the specific topical requests sent me earlier, I spoke on "A Bird's Eye View of the Holy

Land" and "Christian Stewardship." For these two challenging themes I was allotted a full forty minutes!

I remember a preacher whose sermon had become sandwiched between a previous long-winded speaker and a preannounced closing time. Whereas the preacher had been promised thirty minutes, he found he had five. He began his "brief remarks" by saying, "I feel like an Egyptian mummy — pressed for time." I was somewhat pressed for time this morning.

June 2

Although some have suggested a merger of the GKMI and the GITJ, I think it is out of the question. The GITJ is Javanese through and through. The GKMI has a Chinese base and its leadership is still predominantly Chinese. The two groups don't think and operate in the same way.

Typical Javanese procedure is somewhat "laid back" (to use an American term). Haste and impatience are considered unseemly. The Chinese of southeastern Asia are activists; they are always in motion and want results. The Javanese are soft-spoken; the Chinese are more verbally aggressive.

June 3

I have been learning about the work of the Mennonite Central Committee (MCC) in Indonesia. At present its main task is to assist people who are being resettled — "transmigrated" is the customary word — by the government from the overpopulated islands of Java, Bali, and Lombok to more open regions in Sumatra, Kalimantan (Borneo), Sulawesi (Celebes), the Moluccas, and Irian Jaya (western New Guinea). In view of the stark reality that while Java has 7% of Indonesia's land area it has 62% of the population, the government's policy seems to be an economic and political necessity.

The MCC also sponsors workers with special skills. For example, Marian Hooge of Saskatchewan is now preparing to serve in a leprosarium in Irian Jaya. She is a physical therapist, has had training at the United States leprosarium in Carville, Louisiana, and has just finished a period of language study in Bandung, Java. She is intelligent, wholesome, and has a well-used Bible. Also worthy of note is the pattern of MCC financial assistance to both the GITJ and the GKMI.

June 5

This evening I led the last of the three Holy Land seminars at Perkantas (InterVarsity). Large groups of university students were present. I dealt with history and geography and also gave expositions of Amos 9:11-15; Psalm 48, 87, 122; and Hebrews 12:18-29.

These were long sessions — 5 to 9 p.m. each evening, with a break at the halfway point. At about 8:00 tonight my voice became a very unwilling instrument. I was tired — partly from the constant effort to phrase things simply (KISS — keep it simple, Stupid) for the sake of my interpreter, who incidentally was excellent. But Doris tells me it went well. And certainly the Holy Land theme is seldom handled here. Many of the students had never seen Holy Land slides. Some even tried to take flash pictures of slides as they were thrown onto a huge screen. I wished them luck.

June 6

In order to meet our tour group for a one-day junket to Bogor and the tea plantations beyond, we took a taxi at 7:30 a.m. to Hotel Indonesia. But when we got there we found we *were* the "tour group." We were the only ones who had signed up. Panorama Tours however is not without honor, and so at 8:00 the van driver, the official guide, and Doris and I left for Bogor, forty miles to the south.

Even though our guide was knowledgeable and courteous, we were glad that at the great Bogor Botanical Gardens we could roam on our own and explore as we wished. The Gardens are a wonderland of flowers, ponds, pathways, and great trees. At one point the overhanging bamboo bowers have created a shade so dense that even at noon we walked in a dusky green twilight. An old cemetery is there, shrouded by the almost surrealistic half-light. I saw Dutch names on a few of the stones and 1867 on one of them.

After lunch our van took us up into the high hills to the southeast, up into the bright green world of tea plantations. Tightly packed meter-high tea bushes, all neatly clipped and trimmed, covered every hill slope within view. We saw square miles of tea. In long dresses and conical hats, groups of young women were at work at widely separated points, bending over in the task of harvesting and putting the young leaves in sacks.

June 7

This evening Allen Harder and his fiancée took Doris and me to Ancol Park. It contains swimming pools, an art center, sidewalk restaurants, and a stage for Indonesian dances. We swam in a "pool" that is 20 feet wide and that winds its way for hundreds of yards under palm trees around a full 360 degrees. Moreover, it has a clockwise current. It was delightful to swim and float around and around, looking up at the night sky.

Then we ate at a Chinese restaurant under the trees. In spite of the agressiveness of two cats, three blue-bottle flies, and one oversized cockroach (he seemed to walk around on stilts), I enjoyed my Fu Yung Hai. I swatted the flies — they were slow on takeoffs — shooed the cockroach down a tableside drain, and threw ice cubes at the cats.

After the meal we watched several young girls, ages about four to eight, performing Sundanese and Javanese dances. Their costumes were colorful and their movements and gestures graceful and restrained.

As we strolled about we came across a stand where durian fruit was heaped for sale. From 15 feet away I caught my first nose-wrenching whiff. The durian is famous for its dubious odor. Some people however love it. One American fellow said, "It's like eating an ice cream cone in an outhouse." I ate a small chunk but I can't say I liked it. Doris had several pieces. She's a great woman, in spite of a few odd tastes (sauerkraut, olives, durian, and large slabs of raw onion between slices of bread). But then she thinks my taste for buttermilk and yogurt is odd.

On the way home we passed a streetside beggar and Allen began to narrate an experience a North American Mennonite church worker had in Jakarta. When he was accosted by a beggar woman with a baby in her arms, he remonstrated in Indonesian, "Oh come on, you rented that baby for the day" (not an uncommon practice) — whereupon she pulled out a breast and gave him a squirt of milk right in his face!

Mennonites seem to have a way of getting into unusual situations in overseas cities. In Tokyo I heard of a Pennsylvania Mennonite bishop who was innocently strolling on the Ginza when a pimp appeared and offered him a woman. The good bishop had never encountered such a shocking invitation and in his embarrassment offered the lame reply, "I don't have time."

"Doesn't take long," said the pimp. I am pleased to report that the bishop then betook himself away from the scene of enticement.

June 8

Allen spoke last night of Pak Joyo, the GITJ leader. Especially in his young, more vigorous years, he was a great pastor to North Americans who served under the MCC in Indonesia. "Lots of those young fellows owe their spiritual lives to Pak Joyo. . . . A beautiful person. A complex person."

Shortly before bedtime Allen came up to me with a big grin and said, "Now is as good a time as any to tell you. When Wati, my housekeeper, found that you like to take night walks, she gave a 2,000 rupiah tip to the community security people and asked them to take special care of you." So I had unseen protectors. Fascinating.

"Was I really in any danger?" I asked.

"No, she was just being super-careful."

June 9

We were airborne at 10:40 on our flight to Singapore. We had unusual visibility. Twenty minutes after takeoff I looked to the south — directly into Sunda Strait. One or two high mountains reared up to the southeast in western Java, and the Sumatra coastline lay to the southwest. And between Java and Sumatra, far to the south where the strait opens into the Indian Ocean, I believe I saw the island remnants of Krakatoa. There in 1883 occurred the most violent volcanic explosion of modern times. Fourteen cubic miles of debris were flung skyward and the sound was heard 3,000 miles away on Madagascar. SundaStrait was also the scene of a desperate night naval battle in February 1942, in which the USS "Houston" and the Australian cruiser "Perth" were sunk by a superior Japanese force.

We landed at Singapore in late morning and then continued on to Hong Kong and Honolulu. After six days of rest and travel on the islands of Oahu, Maui, and Hawaii, we will fly to San Francisco, Chicago, and Elkhart. There we will be reunited with our family.

About the Author

Stanley Shenk has taught Bible at Eastern Mennonite College and Goshen College. An ordained minister in the Mennonite Church, he has served congregations in Ohio, Pennsylvania, and Indiana. He and his wife Doris have worked together in church assignments in the Middle East and the Far East, in addition to leading a series of tours to the Holy Land. His academic background includes an S.T.B. from Biblical Seminary in New York, a Ph.D. From New York University, and post-doctoral work at Hebrew University in Jerusalem.

Doris Sell Shenk grew up in Souderton, Pa., and attended Eastern Mennonite College. She and Stanley were married in 1942. For 15 years she taught in public and church schools and for ten years she served as administrative assistant to the Dean at Goshen College. In 1980 she received a B.A. in Interdisciplinary Studies from Goshen College. She and Stanley are the parents of four children — and the grandparents of twelve.